CALM
CHRISTMAS
and a HAPPY NEW YEAR

A Little Book of Festive Joy

Beth Kempton

SCRIBNER

New York London Toronto Sydney New Delhi

Scribner

An Imprint of Simon & Schuster, Inc.

1230 Avenue of the Americas

New York, NY 10020

First Scribner hardcover edition October 2020

SCRIBNER and design are registered trademarks of The Gale Group, Inc.,
used under license by Simon & Schuster, Inc., the publisher of this work.

For information about special discounts for bulk purchases,
please contact Simon & Schuster Special Sales at 1-866-506-1949
or business@simonandschuster.com.

The Simon & Schuster Speakers Bureau can bring authors to your live event. For
more information or to book an event, contact the Simon & Schuster Speakers
Bureau at 1-866-248-3049 or visit our website at www.simonspeakers.com.

Manufactured in the United States of America

1   3   5   7   9   10   8   6   4   2

Library of Congress Cataloging-in-Publication Data has been applied for.

ISBN 978-1-9821-5185-0
ISBN 978-1-9821-5187-4 (ebook)

To my parents and brothers,
for teaching me about Christmas magic

To Mr. K, Sienna, and Maia,
for keeping that magic alive

CONTENTS

CONTENTS

PART 3
Manifestation: After Christmas

A Note from the Author

This book is for life, not just for Christmas.

Think of it as a quiet retreat from all the noise, and a guide to honoring a special season without sacrificing your well-being. I hope it inspires connection, belonging, self-care, nourishment, and joy, and a little bit of festive magic.

This collection of stories, advice, and ideas is based in the belief that there is no single way to approach Christmas. It brings together all kinds of Christmases, celebrated in all kinds of ways by all kinds of people.

It's a portrait of us as human beings, pausing in the rush of life to celebrate, to acknowledge those we love and those we miss, to mark the passing of another year, and to make peace and pies, marmalade and memories.

A gentle word of warning—this book offers no military strategy for executing the perfect Christmas. It is more likely to compel you to ditch half your plans and open up space for spontaneity. It will make you question convention and inherited tradition in order to shape a celebration that recognizes what you really need and treasure most.

It will also encourage you to use the precious time between Christmas and New Year's Day to reflect and plan. By the end, instead of heading into January exhausted and lethargic, with lingering dissatisfaction and a credit card hangover, you can go forth feeling rested and rejuvenated, with fresh motivation and a hopeful heart.

The world shifted in 2020, and times have been challenging in many ways. May *Calm Christmas* be a lantern leading you through the darkness of winter, back to the real enchantment of the season. I hope it brings much joy.

Wishing you a Calm Christmas and a Happy New Year.

Beth Kempton
Devon, England, 2020

The Most Wonderful Time of the Year?

ARRIVAL

Of all the scenarios I had imagined for celebrating the first Christmas after my wedding, and the expected birth of our first child on December 11, none of them involved being at a hospital in the middle of a raging storm on Christmas Eve. But then, babies have a habit of sending carefully crafted plans into disarray.

I was supposed to have a lovely home birth, all gentle breathing and candles and a warm birthing pool. But with each passing day beyond our daughter's due date, that home birth started to look less likely, and I could feel my sense of control disintegrating, along with the last vestige of my image of a perfect Christmas.

The vision of us snuggled up with our sleeping newborn by the twinkling lights of the tree—gone.

Opening sweet baby gifts as we sipped mulled wine—gone.

Tucking into the lavish Christmas dinner we had managed to concoct as clever, multitasking new parents—gone.

One by one, the dreams vanished as we edged closer to December 23, when the doctors would insist on inducing.

By the time Christmas Eve rolled in on the wings of that burly storm, I was in a sterile hospital ward with a bag of barbecue-flavor chips, rationing myself to one after each contraction. No Christmas tree, no roast dinner, no presents, no guests, no jolly raising of glasses of bubbly. Just me and my husband . . . and fifteen other pregnant women, all sectioned off behind white plastic curtains, identifiable only by their moans or soft chatter or occasional terrifying screams.

Many hours later, we were moved into a private room for the latter stages of labor. I stood by the wide window overlooking the Brighton seashore and tried to breathe deeply. My breathing was just about the only thing left that I could hope to control, and I watched the sea foam glowing under streetlights and a distant pier. Glancing at the clock,

I realized midnight was approaching. Our baby girl would be born on Christmas Day. And still the thunder raged on.

My ideas about Christmas changed forever that night. Sienna May was born as Chopin played serenely in the background and a giant bolt of lightning cracked across the sky, bringing her and a little Christmas magic into our world.

This was the Christmas that made me a mama. And it was the one that made me realize Christmas never goes quite according to plan.

For some, Christmas is a time of great anticipation, indulgence, and delight. A precious time for feasting and family, togetherness and treats. For others, it's a chance to escape the day-to-day and travel back to a more innocent time. But for many, it is yet another struggle at the end of a difficult year.

Just as there is no one shape of a family, there is no one way to "do" Christmas. Yet we are repeatedly shown the same versions of a "perfect" Christmas in the media. As a result, for many, it has become a time of unrealistic expectations and exhaustion.

The truth is our take on the festive season ebbs and flows as we move through life, as children grow up and move away, as older generations pass and new generations are born. We all approach it from different backgrounds, with our own particular ideas about how it should be.

Christmas is at once almost universally recognized and intensely individual. But while the details may vary, the opportunity for love and light is shared.

I hope *Calm Christmas* will help you reconnect with all that Christmas can be—a source of true joy.

BEGINNINGS

I'm thirteen years old and stumble across a book my mum bought in a rare moment of indulgence. Country Christmas[1] is a large, dark green hardcover. A giant wreath of holly, ivy berries, bay leaves, and tartan ribbons fills the cover. As winter closes in, I reach for that book and curl up to read all about Christmas in the countryside. Calm descends like a gentle snowfall on my early teenage years.

Fast-forward three decades and my mum finds Country

Christmas when rifling through some boxes in her attic. Knowing how much I treasured it as a child, she sends it on to me. As soon as I hold it, and hear the spine creak for the first time in years, I am a teenager again, folded into a deep red armchair, dreaming. The book falls open at a double-page spread of a country cottage at twilight. Stone walls strong beneath a navy sky, fairy lights clustered on a tree outside, candles in every window to welcome home the children jostling by the front door. In bobble hats and winter coats, they are just back from sleighing, I presume.

That single photograph held so much for me as a teenager. It was everything I wanted from my adult life—a family of my own, a solid old house to call home, warmth, comfort, and safety. Sitting at my kitchen table now, at the heart of our five-hundred-year-old cottage, I reflect on the decisions and sacrifices that have led me from that book to this room. Only now do I realize how powerful my association with Christmas—and that specific image—has been over the years.

When we try to describe our favorite parts of the festivities, we often talk about the tangible aspects, like "my aunt's roast potatoes" or "the twinkling lights on the trees." These are precious personal details, but I believe they sit on the surface of something more profound. Many of us have a generations-deep connection to the season, often shaped by childhood. When we think of Christmas, the image we conjure up, and the feelings that flood back, might just as easily reflect what we secretly longed for as what we *actually* experienced, even if the two were very different. It is by reconnecting with what we loved or yearned for as children that we can find true joy in the midst of the darkest season.

> *Christmas is a microcosm of our lives—*
> *both the rough and the smooth come into focus.*

I have spent Christmas with a heart full of anticipation as a child; warming my hands by a temperamental electric fire deep in the mountains of northern Japan as an exchange student; sunburnt on a boat crossing the equator in my twenties; and, most memorably, in a hospital giving birth to my elder daughter. I have been overjoyed, overwhelmed, stressed, relaxed, cold, hot, happy, sad, feeling loved, feeling lonely, surrounded by family, thousands of miles from family, single, married, before children, with children. With each passing year I am more aware of how much I enjoy simplicity, and a calm Christmas is usually a good Christmas, which leads into a happier New Year.

My love of Christmas is legendary in our family, with October bringing half-joking/half-serious questions about whether the carols have been played yet (they usually have). But there have been years when my favorite festival has lost its sparkle, tarnished by in-your-face commercialism and the pressure to fit elaborate preparations into our already busy lives.

When our children came along, my husband and I started to think more about what kind of Christmas we wanted to weave into their childhoods, and how we might craft a celebration that would leave us all feeling full of love, gratitude, and energy. Ultimately, this meant having some tough conversations, letting go of perfection, and finding new ways to honor the most important of our two families' traditions.

The first step was to strip it all back and discover what "Christmas" truly meant to us, then find ways to match that with the expectations of our friends and loved ones. We also wanted to preserve a calm space in the middle of it all in which we could rest and prepare ourselves for the year ahead.

The experiment that followed over the next few years became a calmer approach to Christmas, and the bones of this book.

THE CASE FOR A NEW KIND OF CHRISTMAS

I'll let you in on a secret. With all the turmoil our world has seen this year, there have been times when I have wondered if a book about Christmas is a frivolous indulgence. But when I started to look into the science of the season—the data on stress levels going through the roof, growing numbers of people suffering from Christmas-related mental health issues, and the mountain of debt created by rampant commercialization and overindulgence—it soon became clear that this is a very serious business, and that changing the way we approach it could have a transformational effect on our general well-being and outlook, particularly after the year we have just had.

Christmas, which is the single most widely celebrated festival in the world, is considered so important that we shell out a staggering $1 trillion each Christmas.[2] So it is hardly surprising that almost two-thirds of us find the holiday season stressful.[3]

Nevertheless, year in, year out, millions of people approach it in the same old way—huge buildup, mounting panic, followed by a massive energy crash. Even those of us who adore Christmas often take on far too much, giving everything to others and leaving nothing for ourselves.

We are missing a vital opportunity to relax, reconnect, and be rejuvenated by this very special season, simply because of what we have come to believe about how it *should* be. But when we smother our true desires with brandy butter and silence, we end up making the same mistakes year after year.

It's time for a new kind of festive season, one that allows us to create magic and memories without sacrificing our own well-being, ushering us towards a lasting sense of serenity and contentment.

Some notes about . . .

RELIGION

In this book I share my experiences of the religious aspects of Christmas within the context of my own childhood, and now as a parent of young children. I went to Sunday school and attended a church school from the age of ten, so the religious side of Christmas was always a significant part of the story for me. From Nativity plays to carol services, Advent candles to Christingle oranges, the local church was integral to my experience of the season, but Christmas does not have to be connected to religion. Indeed, almost half of the Americans who celebrate Christmas do not even consider it a religious holiday.[4]

Writing this book has given me a wonderful opportunity to explore traditions—my own, those in wider culture, and those held dear by the hundreds of people I have connected with in the course of my research. I have heard the Christmas memories of people from several generations, thirty-seven nationalities, and every corner of the world. People who identify with several different religions, as well as atheists and many who are not really sure where their faith lies, have shared their stories with me. We are united by the fact that we carry the magic of the season close to our hearts.

GEOGRAPHY

The seasonal aspects of this book are based in the northern hemisphere, where Christmas falls in midwinter, which is often dark, wet, and cold. However, I also share some stories from the southern hemisphere, where Christmas is experienced in the summer, usually in bright sunshine and heat. Wherever in the world you are based, I hope you will find comfort and inspiration for enjoying the festivities and transitioning gently into January.

THE CHRISTMAS TIMELINE

In many English-speaking countries, Christmas is primarily celebrated with feasting on December 25. If your main celebration falls on a different day, you can simply adjust your preparations accordingly.

UNWRAPPING THIS BOOK

I hope this book will liberate you from any stifling inherited traditions that no longer align with your values, and encourage you to keep only those you treasure. And I hope it will inspire you to create your own kind of Christmas, based on what matters to you and those you love.

Divided into three parts that span the buildup, the festivities themselves, and the days that follow, this book embraces the full breadth of the holiday season in a holistic, nurturing way.

In Part 1, "Anticipation," I will whisk you away from the frenetic energy of the high street and invite you to sit awhile, next to the roaring fire in my kitchen, hot chocolate in hand, where we will explore the meaning of Christmas. Then we will reimagine what the season can be before working out how to plan and prepare for a calm experience, filled with pockets of delight. Next we will flow with the energy of nature at this time of year, aligning with the natural rhythms that nourish mind, body, and spirit and carry us through winter.

In Part 2, "Celebration," we will lose ourselves in the wonder of everything Christmas, from mindful gifting to festive gatherings. We will explore how to radiate calm at this time of year by abandoning ideas of perfection, finding peace in the chaos, and giving ourselves permission to step away whenever it all gets a bit too much. Then we will honor the melancholy that often accompanies the season, stemming from loneliness, sadness, and grief, and find ways to acknowledge our feelings while still making space for joy.

In Part 3, "Manifestation," we will discover a fresh approach to planning for a fulfilling, inspiring year ahead. After exploring an abundance of ways to savor the days between Christmas and New Year's Day, we will reflect on the year that is coming to an end. Finally, I will share a host of tools for envisioning a positive future and offer advice on how to make that dream a reality, before we walk together through the gateway of New Year's Eve and into a gentle January and beyond.

Along the way there will be many opportunities for you to reflect and plan, and I encourage you to make notes in a journal or scribble in the margins of this book.

Any time you feel frazzled or stressed, remember you can always turn to these pages for solace. You're always welcome here, beside me at my kitchen table. There are logs on the fire, tea in the pot, and cinnamon buns fresh out of the oven.

Pull up a chair and relax. It is Christmas, after all.

PART 1

Anticipation:
Before Christmas

CHAPTER 1

The Five Stories of Christmas

GETTING TO THE HEART
OF CHRISTMAS

What image makes you pause a moment and realize that Christmas is on its way? The first robin appearing in the hedgerow? The blurred reflection of Christmas lights in puddles on the road? The scent of cinnamon and cloves? Woodsmoke in the air? A good mood, riding on the shoulders of passersby?

We all have our markers, and when we catch a glimpse of one, inhale the aroma of another, and sense the arrival of a third, our brain stitches all of the pieces together and whispers, "Christmas is coming."

When I hear the word "Christmas," I see a personal movie reel in my mind's eye. And your own reel probably starts running, too. But that doesn't mean we are watching the same show. Therein lies the challenge we face when sharing Christmas with other people. We all expect different things, often without even realizing it.

If you find yourself insisting that Christmas has "lost all meaning," it may be that you feel caught up in a story that you consider unimportant or trivial, rather than one you value. Or perhaps you are inadvertently judging other people's notions of Christmas through your own lens. This mismatch of expectation and reality can be a real source of stress and resentment at this time of year, and it is the main obstacle we have to overcome in order to experience a calmer, more joyful Christmas.

I became curious about which symbols of Christmas are universal, as I thought they may give us something to rally around. As I dug deeper into my research, I was surprised to learn that not one single element of the stereotypical Christmas is invariably applicable. Not everyone puts up a Christmas tree, or sings carols, or hopes for snow, or cooks a turkey, or exchanges gifts, or gathers with others to celebrate.

Nevertheless, there is a pool of experiences from which we all seem to draw at least one memory that is closely associated with the season, often related to our senses. The sights, sounds, smells, tastes, and textures of Christmases past linger in our hearts and inform our ideas of what it should be in the future.

In the course of my research, I also discovered that the roots of our traditions are deeply buried in legend and lore, and that it is extremely hard to unearth accurate facts about the origins of Christmas. The history of this most famous holiday is littered with so many contradictions, assumptions, and unverifiable assertions that getting to the truth of it all is challenging.

Even the duration of Christmas is up for discussion. Some people start with the lighting of the first Advent candle—four Sundays before Christmas—and run through to Twelfth Night (January 5) on the eve of the Epiphany. Others begin with the winter solstice (somewhere between December 20 and 23, depending on the year) and honor the old tradition of Yule in early January. For yet others, the Christmas season starts with the Black Friday sales the day after Thanksgiving (which falls on the fourth Thursday each November) and ends with collapsing onto the sofa surrounded by discarded wrapping paper on Christmas Day. And some people manage to compress the whole thing into three days of mayhem and indulgence from Christmas Eve to Boxing Day (December 26), based around when the office is closed.

Our Christmas timelines, along with our food, decorations, and activities, vary according to culture and generation. Some people love the flurry and bustle of Christmas, while others resent the retail-led nature of the season and would rather spend it in peace.

In speaking to people from all walks of life, of all ages and backgrounds, I discovered one salient truth: every Christmas is unique. Each one is a carefully constructed, complex narrative that has formed as Christmas has whirled across time and geography, down family lineages, through television and social media feeds, and around our kitchen tables. No two are ever the same, either from year to year or from person to person. We need to slow down and get up close to see the complex and particular beauty of each one.

THE FIVE STORIES OF CHRISTMAS

Everyone I asked seemed to value and identify with at least one of five essential stories of Christmas. These are tales of faith, magic, connection, abundance, and heritage that have been told and retold for generations. Our personal connection to each of them offers a snapshot of what Christmas means to us at a particular moment in our lives. They provide clues to the triggers for our stress and the sources of our joy. They offer a framework for understanding our individual, deep-rooted views of Christmas, and discerning what to hold on to and what to release.

Even more importantly, viewing Christmas through the lens of these five stories can increase our understanding of each other, which can have a monumental, positive impact on our shared experience. By understanding what matters most to ourselves and those close to us, we can organize our gatherings, prepare our hearts, and strengthen our resolve to give and take just enough to ensure a calm, joyful Christmas for everyone.

21

So, with open minds and a stocking full of curiosity, let's dive into the five stories of Christmas.

NOTE: *At the end of each of the five stories, I will ask you to reflect on your degree of connection to it and its influence on your interpretation of Christmas. Some of the stories might resonate deeply, others not at all. Be honest, and write what you really think. There are no right or wrong answers as everyone's Christmas is different.*

THE STORY OF FAITH

The biblical Christmas story,[1] which is celebrated in cathedrals, churches, and chapels and acted out every year by millions of small children in tinsel headdresses the world over, might be considered the archetypal Christmas Story of Faith. It is instantly recognizable from a number of details: no room at the inn; a baby born in a manger wrapped in swaddling clothes; a bright star in the sky. When you look closely, it is a fantastical, powerful tale of dreams and intuition, greed and fear, generosity and wonder, perseverance and joy.

Here is a summary of this famous story as I have come to know it, with some of the finer points omitted for brevity. Forgive me if the version you know differs a little.

Long, long ago (about two millennia back), far, far away (in Judea, to the west of the Dead Sea), God sent an angel (Gabriel) to visit a young woman by the name of Mary. She lived in the town of Nazareth and was engaged to marry a carpenter named Joseph. Gabriel told Mary that she would become pregnant by the Holy Spirit and give birth to a baby boy, who was God's own son. She should name him Jesus (which some translate as "Savior").

At the time, Judea was part of the Roman Empire, and the Emperor Augustus ordered a census of the population to ensure everyone was up to date with their taxes. This meant that Mary and Joseph had to travel to Joseph's hometown of Bethlehem.

When they finally arrived, every lodging house was full. After knocking on many doors and being turned away, they finally found a friendly innkeeper who offered them the use of his stable. After such a long journey, the shelter was a relief, and it was there that Jesus was born. He was wrapped in swaddling clothes and laid in a manger filled with hay.

On the hills around Bethlehem, angels appeared to a group of shepherds to tell them the good news: the Son of God had been born in the town that night. The shepherds went to visit Jesus, and told everyone about their visitation. At the same time, a bright star appeared in the sky. It was spotted from far away by a trio of Wise Men, who had read that a new star would appear when a great king was born. They decided to follow the star and pay homage to the new king.

The Wise Men eventually arrived at the stable and bowed down to the baby, offering gifts of gold, frankincense, and myrrh.

When you dig into the details of this story, there are countless gray areas and seeming inaccuracies. For instance, according to the historical record, the census was held in AD 6, some six years after Mary and Joseph supposedly made the trip to Bethlehem. There are also questions regarding why shepherds were tending their sheep in the fields at the end of December, and why the heavily pregnant Mary traveled to Bethlehem with her husband, given that women were not included in

Roman censuses.[2] Regardless, the story is undeniably captivating, which is why it has survived for so many generations and spread so far across the world.

It was a fourth-century bishop of Rome who first proclaimed December 25 to be the date of Jesus Christ's Nativity. Since then, many other church-based traditions and rituals have developed around the day itself, including the lighting of Advent candles, bell ringing, Midnight Mass, and, of course, the singing of Christmas carols. Many famous carols retell aspects of the Nativity story, whereas others focus on hardship, generosity, and a sense of shared humanity in the bleakest part of the year.

I will never forget my elder daughter's first candle-lit carol service in the tiny village church, her little heart bursting with pride as she declared that it was "Busy, busy, busy in Bethlehem today." The centuries-old stone building was swollen with sweet voices and a cloud of mulled wine as the carols swirled in the cold night air.

While some places still sing traditional carols that date back hundreds of years—such as the sixteenth-century "Coventry Carol"—most of the familiar ones were written much later than that.[3] Nevertheless, when you join with other voices on a dark December night, you step into a continuum of communal Christmas spirit that flows through the ages.

According to the late Stephen Cleobury, former director of music at King's College, Cambridge:

> Those who have been nurtured in this tradition but who have in one way or another departed from it can still respond at this special time of year to the retelling of the Christmas story. Many who have no faith or who come from other religious traditions can be deeply moved by the combinations of words and music, which, at the simplest level, tell the human story of the birth of a young child.[4]

So, here we are in the twenty-first century, many of us grappling with what to make of the Story of Faith. Ponder your own personal connection to it and the role it has played in your Christmases over the years.

CALM CONTEMPLATION:
FAITH

- Which parts of the Story of Faith do you connect with the most? Why? How do you feel when you think about them?
- Do you have a specific memory that is related to the Story of Faith?
- What is your personal Story of Faith? How does it relate to Christmas, if at all?
- Is there anything about the Story of Faith (including expectations connected to it) that you find stressful or otherwise challenging?
- On a scale of 1 to 10, how important is faith to you at Christmas?

THE STORY OF MAGIC

It's Christmas Eve, and at the North Pole a jolly, plump, bearded old man is pulling on a velvety red suit, edged with white fur. He fastens the gold buckle on his wide black belt and pats his belly with both hands as he checks his reflection in the long wooden mirror. He peers at his face and wonders if his cheeks are looking pinker than usual this year. There are a few extra wrinkles, but really he's doing rather well for his age.

"Father Christmas! It's nearly time!" one of his elves calls to him from the workshop, where hundreds of others are gathering the last of the presents to pile onto the wooden sleigh.

The old man nods, takes one last sip of steaming hot chocolate from his favorite mug for a little warmth on the long journey that lies ahead, and strides into the take-off area. His sleigh is looking marvelous tonight. The golden frame is glowing. His reindeer are grunting excitedly, looking well-fed and ready for a midnight dash around the world.

An elf runs over and hands the old man the list. The scroll is longer than ever this year.

"Mostly 'nice,' I'm glad to see," Father Christmas says with a wink as he climbs into the driver's seat. He takes the reins and, in a cloud of silvery dust, he is off.

I grew up with this particular Story of Magic. Later, I learned that there were many alternative versions. Some children believed that Father Christmas resided in Lapland, while others insisted his headquarters were in Greenland or northern Canada. Some knew him as Santa Claus, while others had heard that he lived with an equally jolly wife, Mrs. Claus, who supervised the gift making. But we all agreed on one detail: as long as we had been good throughout the year and were fast asleep when he arrived, the big man and his reindeer would land on the roof of each house, then pop down the chimney (or through a window for those who lived in flats) with a sackful of presents. He would leave the gifts in stockings and under the tree, down a glass of sherry, eat a sweet treat and gather up any carrots left out for his reindeer, then shoot back up the chimney (or out the window) and head off to the next house.

As a child, I adored everything about this story. The snow, the elves' workshop, the promise of hooves clattering on the roof and reindeer flying through the sky. And, of course, the mound of presents when we awoke on Christmas morning.

It's difficult to trace the exact origins of the legend of Father Christmas, and, like all the best stories, it evolves with the telling. It is likely that the version I know was forged, in part at least, by the imaginations of screenwriters and film directors who have presented it in a plethora of Christmas movies. But there is some historical basis for it too, albeit a debated one,[5] which leads us all the way back to fourth-century Turkey and the bishop of Myra, who was later canonized as Saint Nicholas.[6]

The story goes that Nicholas was a wealthy man, having inherited a fortune from his parents, but he was kind and generous with it. One day, he heard of a poor man with three daughters who were unable to marry their sweethearts because their father could not afford their dowries. Nicholas wanted to help but also remain anonymous, so he dropped a bag of gold down the chimney in the middle of the night, whereupon it fell into a stocking that the eldest daughter had hung to dry by the fire. He then did the same for the second and third daughters. However, on the third occasion, the father caught Nicholas in the act and was finally able to offer his sincere thanks. In time, after many other kind acts, Nicholas was made a saint, and ever since, children have hung up stockings in the hope that he might look kindly on them, too.

There are countless different names for the lead character in this story, ranging from Père Noël (France) to Sinterklaas (Holland), and the date when he dispenses his gifts varies too, but the heart of the tale is always the same.[7]

The story spans the realms of the real world and the imagination. It connects behavior to reward in the minds of young children and reassures them that someone else, in addition to a parent or guardian, is always looking out for them. And it is enchanting. Who doesn't love the idea of flying reindeer?

CALM CONTEMPLATION: MAGIC

- Where did your ideas about Saint Nicholas/ Father Christmas/Santa Claus come from?
- Did you enjoy other magical stories as a child?
- What is your view of magic—in any form—these days?
- Do you have a specific memory that is related to the Story of Magic?
- Is there anything about this Story of Magic (including any expectations connected to it) that you find stressful or otherwise challenging?

- On a scale of 1 to 10, how important are magic
  and wonder to you at Christmas?

THE STORY OF CONNECTION

In 1843, a well-known English writer by the name of
Charles Dickens published a new novel. The observa-
tions and morals he presented in those pages have gone
on to inform Christmases around the world ever since.
The novel in question was *A Christmas Carol*, and the
story goes something like this:

*One bitter Christmas Eve, a tight-fisted, mean-spirited
old man called Ebenezer Scrooge is unkind to his loyal clerk,
Bob Cratchit, refuses to give money to charity, and is rude
to his nephew, who has invited him over for Christmas.*

*That night, Scrooge is visited by the ghost of his former
business partner, Jacob Marley, and then by three more spirits. The Ghost of Christmas Past takes Scrooge back in time
so that he may see himself as an unhappy child, then as a
young man who is more interested in money than love. The
Ghost of Christmas Present reveals Bob Cratchit's family,
where the smallest child—Tiny Tim—is in poor health but*

full of Christmas cheer, and then his nephew, whose invitation he so rudely declined. Finally, the Ghost of Christmas Future—the most terrifying of all—shows Scrooge visions of his own death.

Through these visitations, Scrooge comes to realize what really matters. He wakes up on Christmas Day, buys an enormous turkey for Bob Cratchit and his family, then enjoys a jolly Christmas with his nephew.

This story is very close to my heart. I remember staying up late one year to help make a costume for my older brother's portrayal of Bob Cratchit in the school play. We dug out an old knitted vest from the back of our dad's closet, tore holes in the knees of his school trousers, and bent some wire into the shape of horn-rimmed glasses. The outfit was completed with a pair of fingerless gloves, to keep his hands warm in Scrooge's unheated office. I must have read or watched *A Christmas Carol* at least a dozen times over the years—on paper, in my brother's school production, on professional stages, and in the Disney cartoon.[8]

If you dig into historical records of Christmas, there is a clear distinction between how it was celebrated until the mid-nineteenth century (when Thomas Kibble

Hervey's *The Book of Christmas*[9] and *A Christmas Carol* were both published) and thereafter. Samuel Pepys's seventeenth-century diaries reveal a focus on church-going (morning *and* evening) and food. For instance, in 1662, he tells us that his Christmas meal consisted of plum porridge, roasted pullet, and a mince pie.[10] Little changed for a couple of centuries, but then many of the traditions we still hold dear today were invented, one after another, over the course of a few short years at the start of Queen Victoria's reign. Before long, these customs were wholly absorbed into popular culture.

It seems that *A Christmas Carol*, which was published just nine years after Christmas Day became a designated national holiday in England, was not so much an account of the typical Christmas but the catalyst for a new kind of festive sentimentality. It gained immense popularity internationally, especially after Dickens undertook a series of promotional tours in the United States, which was in the midst of a transition towards a new kind of Christmas celebration.

A Christmas Carol is a tale of humanity, generosity, fear, family, and second chances. But when you look closely at the story—and at the wider Victorian Christmas that was the setting for the novel—you quickly realize that the principal theme is connection. People gather, share food and time, and display their gratitude towards each other. Indeed, several of the traditions that help us connect—or reconnect—with friends and family at this time of year have their origins precisely when Dickens was writing his story.

In 1843, an inventor by the name of Henry Cole commissioned the artist John Callcott Horsley to design the world's very first Christmas card.[11] It bears the greeting "A Merry Christmas and a Happy New Year to You" and features a jolly gathering of people toasting the festivities. It was another three decades before the first Christmas card originating in the US appeared, in 1875.[12] Some say the modern Christmas card industry did not really begin until 1915, when a Kansas City–based postcard printing company, the Hall Brothers, created its first holiday card, and soon adopted a new format of a folded card in an envelope. A decade later the company changed its name to Hallmark, and now offers over two thousand designs. A century on, and more than 1.3 billion holiday cards are exchanged in the US each year.[13]

Then we have the introduction of the indoor Christmas tree, which rapidly became a central symbol of Christmas for millions of families. It is thought that the first Christmas tree—which was decorated with apples, wafers, and gingerbread—was erected in Freiberg, Germany, as long ago as 1419.[14] Thereafter, other Central European towns, cities, and countries gradually adopted the tradition. Prince Albert is often credited with bringing the idea to Britain, but it actually arrived in the 1790s, when Queen Charlotte, the German wife of George III, decorated a tree for their children.[15] Members of the royal family continued the custom into the new century, so Victoria was familiar with Christmas trees from her childhood.

In 1848, *The Illustrated London News* printed a picture of Victoria and Albert and their children enjoying Christmas at Windsor Castle.[16] The image features a tree bedecked with lit candles and simple decorations while the young royals gaze at it in wonder. It was this picture, and the joy it evoked, that prompted so many ordinary British families to decorate trees in their own homes from the following year onwards. And before long the custom had made its way across the Atlantic.

President Franklin Pierce installed a tree in the White House in 1856, and trees were being sold at Washington Square Park in New York by the 1870s.[17]

These days, the Christmas tree connects us to each other through rituals of decorating, singing, and opening presents beneath it. But it also allows us to reconnect with ourselves, as the American painter Jennifer Ray explains: "As much as I love sharing the time with my family, my very favorite thing to do is to spend a few evenings when everyone has gone to sleep, sitting with the lights off, staring at the twinkling Christmas tree and savoring the magic of Christmas."

This Story of Connection manifests itself in many different ways. For some, it is embodied in a deep love of feasting. For others, it's about generosity and gift-giving. For yet others, it's linked to treasuring family bonds, which are strengthened through collective experiences at Christmastime. The Story of Connection continues with trees to gather around, cards to send, and feasts to share. It's an opportunity to reconnect with loved ones and toast love, life, and the year gone by.

CALM CONTEMPLATION:
CONNECTION

- Do you have a specific memory that is related to a Christmas tree, a Christmas feast, or a particular Christmas gathering?
- Is there anything about the Story of Connection (including any expectations connected to it) that you find stressful or otherwise challenging?
- On a scale of 1 to 10, how important are connection, gathering, and feasting to you?

THE STORY OF ABUNDANCE

The fourth Christmas story is one of abundance—of showering loved ones with gifts and sharing our good fortune with others. It's typified by neighborhood illuminations, the festive pop songs that echo through shopping malls, the Christmas versions of everything from socks to doughnuts, slippers to cat food, the hot dog stands garlanded with tinsel and fundraising Santas on the streets of New York, gingerbread lattes in red cups, and garish Christmas sweaters.

The volume has steadily increased on this Story of Abundance since the 1920s as department stores, television executives, advertising agencies, and social media influencers have all seized this annual opportunity to maximize their profits. Indeed, the current retail-led version of Christmas would be unrecognizable to our great-grandparents.

Back then, Christmas requests were a lot simpler than today. In 2018, a 120-year-old letter to Santa was discovered inside a book donated to a charity shop in England. In neat, looped handwriting, five-year-old Marjorie asks for a piece of ribbon, a ball for her cat Kittykins, and a canvas stocking.[18]

By contrast, while some families today plan to give only a handful of carefully considered gifts, some gift fifty or more presents to each child.[19]

Some people deride this as rampant commercialism. Others enjoy nothing more than piling brightly wrapped gifts around the tree. Although personally I think gift-giving has gone too far, there is no right or wrong way to embrace the Story of Abundance.

The key is to work out which elements of the modern Christmas bring you genuine joy and cherish them, then let go of the rest, rather than get sucked into the materialistic whirlwind.

There are many positive aspects to the Story of Abundance. After all, "abundance" is a generous word. There can be a sense of fun and community spirit in all of this. There is perhaps no better time to share the bounty of our labors than over Christmas, and it can be a true joy to see loved ones opening a gift they adore. We can choose to support creative, independent manufacturers and small businesses through our purchases. Window-shopping to view the handiwork of talented merchandisers can be a delight. Wandering through a traditional Christmas market, hot *glühwein* in hand, perusing handmade crafts and soaking up the festive atmosphere can be a wonderful way to spend a wet evening in December.

But the Story of Abundance also has a dark side of excess, materialism, greed, and waste. It is up to each of

40

us to grapple with that, and settle somewhere that feels authentic, responsible, and good.

CALM CONTEMPLATION: ABUNDANCE

- What elements of the more commercial side of Christmas do you recall from your childhood? Which aspects did you find exciting (such as a particular television ad, the idea of stockings bursting with gifts, writing a letter to Santa, etc.)?
- What is your view of giving (and receiving) gifts today?
- How do you feel about Christmas shopping?
- Is there anything about the Story of Abundance (including any expectations connected to it) that you find stressful or otherwise challenging?
- On a scale of 1 to 10, how important is the celebration of abundance (by way of Christmas shopping, gifting, etc.) to you?

THE STORY OF HERITAGE

This is your family's heirloom version of Christmas, the one that's been handed down to you; and, if you have a partner, perhaps blended with theirs. It is a carefully strained composite of all the geographical, ethnic, and cultural influences you have received, grown up with, or adopted over the course of many years—the inherited treasures and quirky traditions that link you directly to your family and childhood. Perhaps you follow your great-grandmother's secret strudel recipe each year. Or sing a particular song every Christmas morning. Or haul a Yule log into the house. Or hang out the stocking your father used as a child. Or step outside before bedtime on Christmas Eve to soak up the cool, winter air, just as you have every year since you were fifteen.

Depending on where your family hails from, or where you live now, you may have been exposed to local folklore that has been passed down over centuries.

Some people like to honor pagan midwinter rites,

while others focus on the local climate or on how their families celebrated Christmas in years gone by.

Remember, though, that tradition is not the same as convention. The former encompasses a degree of commitment—you have to want to keep tradition alive—whereas the latter relates to organizing things in a certain manner simply because they've always been done that way. So the Story of Heritage involves *choosing* to recognize, honor, and uphold certain traditions.

The depth and variety of people's versions of this story are apparent in the following recollections from around the world:

> I celebrate the winter solstice and love walking in the woods and the countryside on a clear, crisp morning. I love fairy lights, candles, being indoors by the fire, the scent of cinnamon, spices, delicious food, reading for hours, time to slow down. Time to hibernate and look within.
>
> —Cristina, France

> My abiding memory of Christmas in Africa is the abundance of gorgeous red flame lilies that grew all

43

around our farm. We would go out and pick huge bunches to have in the house.

> —Linda, reflecting on her
> childhood in Zimbabwe

Before we moved to the Middle East, Christmas meant darkness, fairy lights, snow, real Christmas trees, and chilly walks. Now Christmas means the best photo light and sunny weather, fires in the garden, fake Christmas trees of all colors, Arabic food, travel, and swimming.

> —Ellen, Bahrain

We always pick a country and cook a big, fancy meal in that cuisine for Christmas Eve. My partner is Jewish, so we also celebrate Hanukkah together and light candles. It's a beautiful combination of our traditions. Both are about bringing light into life, so it feels lovely.

> —Laura, United States

Summer. Prawns. Mangoes. Champagne. Time off work. Long, lazy days. Meaningful celebrations.

Discarding anything that does not feel authentic and wholehearted.

—Rebecca, Australia

To me, Christmas is family, ritual, bonding, raising the drawbridge and shutting out the world to escape into a place outside of time.

—Emma, UK

CALM CONTEMPLATION: HERITAGE

- What is your view of traditions related to mid-winter, such as decorating your home with evergreens and celebrating the winter solstice? Are these parts of your Christmas story?
- What sort of weather do you associate with Christmas? What impact does it have on how you expect to feel and what you do at this time of year?
- What other elements of Christmas are important to you? What particular traditions have been

handed down through your family and become part of your personal Christmas story? (Some of these might cross over with stories one through four.) How do you feel about them? Do you want to maintain them or not?

- Do you have one particular memory associated with Christmas and your family's heritage?
- What impact do your particular life stage and current circumstances have on how you think of Christmas?
- Is there anything about the Story of Heritage (including any expectations connected to it) that you find stressful or otherwise challenging?
- On a scale of 1 to 10, how important are inherited family traditions, or those you have created yourself, at Christmas?

WRITING YOUR CHRISTMAS STORY

To invite a calmer, more joyful celebration, look closely at the narrative you have built around Christmas and take ownership of it, or rewrite it.

When we think about what Christmas means to us, we recall both individual memories and an overarching narrative. We inherit much of the narrative, but also build on it as we go through life, making various decisions about whom to share it with, where to spend it, and how to celebrate. So our own narrative evolves and influences those of others around us. In this way, it becomes part of our legacy.

Much of the stress of Christmas comes from either not giving ourselves permission to evolve our inherited narrative, or from the pressure to evolve it into something that is out of alignment with what, deep down, we believe about Christmas. The more stressful we allow it to become, the less time we have to create new memorable moments and tune in to what should be the most joyful time of the year.

What we need is a way to marry what matters to us with what matters to those we love, and then let go of the rest.

CHAPTER 2

Mission: Christmas

THE CHRISTMAS CONSTELLATION

For me, Christmas planning used to involve an hour or two in a cozy café in mid-November, perhaps with some gentle jazz playing in the background, a fresh pot of tea, and some ginger cake. I'd have pen, paper, and a calendar, and I would settle down to write my lists.

These days, there is one major difference. Before I start listing everything I must do, I check in with my Christmas Constellation. This is a powerful tool I developed for inviting a calmer Christmas, and it has transformed not only the way I plan but also my enjoyment of the festive season, so I hope you will give it a try.

How to Create Your Very Own Christmas Constellation

1. Copy the following chart on a double-page spread in your notebook, or download the template from dowhatyouloveforlife.com/course/cc.

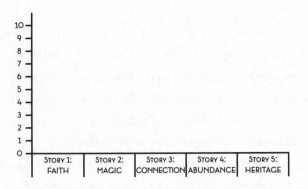

2. Go back to your answers to the Calm Contemplation questions in Chapter 1 and note down your score from the final question (out of 10) for each story. It's fine to have rated more than one story highly, even if doing so seems a bit contradictory. Clement Clarke

Moore, author of "A Visit from St. Nicholas," that famous poem about the night before Christmas, was a very religious man and a professor at the General Theological Seminary in New York City,[1] so he probably would have scored Story 1 *and* Story 2 as a 9 or a 10.

However, if you find that you have scored *all* the stories very highly, try to identify which you relate to the *most* and adjust accordingly. Very few of us love every aspect of Christmas equally; and even if we do, trying to commit to each of them equally is likely to be a source of significant stress. If you are a little more strict with your ratings, you will find your Constellation becomes a much more useful tool. Here's an example:

Gloria was brought up in a religious family, and although she doesn't go to church regularly anymore, she still considers Christmas to be a religious holiday, loves traditional carols, and always attends Midnight Mass on Christmas Eve. She is sad that few people now make this connection and feels that Christmas has lost some of its meaning as a result. She has no problem with the emphasis on Father Christmas, but she has no children of her own, so she doesn't think about it too much.

51

What matters most to her is gathering her parents, her siblings, and their families at her home for a feast. She enjoys the Christmas lights in her town but feels stressed out by crowds and dislikes the constant pressure to buy gifts for distant relatives and acquaintances. She has fun decorating her house with holly and ivy and lighting candles, just as her grandmother and great-grandmother did before her.

Gloria might score her stories as follows:

- Importance of the Story of Faith = strong (8)
- Importance of the Story of Magic = weak (2)
- Importance of the Story of Connection = very strong (9)
- Importance of the Story of Abundance = fairly weak (3)
- Importance of the Story of Heritage = fairly strong (7)

3. Now plot all five of your scores on the chart, using stars. As an example, Gloria's Christmas Constellation would look like this:

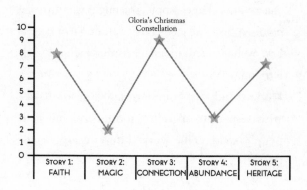

Gloria's idea of Christmas is immediately obvious, and a quick glance at the chart will help her to:

- Recognize what she wants to honor and celebrate over the Christmas period (primarily faith, connection, and heritage). In turn, this will give her a good idea of which invitations to accept as well as who and what to seek out over the holidays.
- Realize that the Stories of Magic and Abundance—in other words, the concept of Santa Claus and the commercial side of Christmas—are relatively unimportant to her.
- Tune in to one of the three stories that bring her

the most joy. For example, she might want to play carols, drop some iced cookies around to a neighbor, or share a childhood Christmas memory with a friend.

- Understand the boundaries she needs to set with respect to spending too much time with people who value very different aspects of Christmas.

CALM CONTEMPLATION: YOUR CHRISTMAS CONSTELLATION

Consult your Christmas Constellation and think about what it is telling you, then jot down your responses to the following questions.

- Which of the five stories pull you outwards, to other people, and which pull you inwards, to yourself? Which one feels particularly important right now?
- What, specifically, do you want and need to honor within your celebrations this year? This

does not have to be on Christmas Day itself; it can be any time during the season.

• What do you want to avoid this year? How might you achieve this?

PLOTTING A LOVED ONE'S CHRISTMAS CONSTELLATION

Things get even more interesting when we look at the Christmas Constellations of the people we are likely to spend the most time with over the holidays. Let's return to our earlier example of Gloria:

Gloria's husband, Nick, isn't religious, but he enjoys hearing the carols Gloria plays at home. He feels Christmas is a magical time of year that is brought to life by a jolly old elf, and he likes putting up a Christmas tree. He enjoys handing out special gifts while wearing a Santa hat, but he detests the media circus, thinks that people spend far too much money on junk, and gets upset by all the waste. He loves maintaining the traditions he has inherited, including midwinter celebrations and cooking old family recipes.

Nick might score his stories as follows:

- Importance of the Story of Faith = weak (2)
- Importance of the Story of Magic = very strong (9)
- Importance of the Story of Connection = fairly strong (7)
- Importance of the Story of Abundance = fairly weak (3)
- Importance of the Story of Heritage = very strong (9)

If we plot these scores on Nick's chart, his Christmas Constellation looks like this:

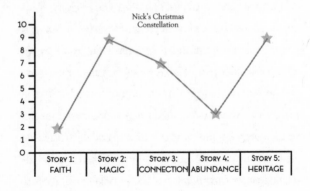

56

This will help Nick to:

- Recognize what he wants to honor over the Christmas period (primarily the magic of Christmas and his own heritage, followed by connections to other people).
- Realize that the Stories of Faith and Abundance (the religious and commercial aspects of Christmas) are unimportant to him.
- Tune in to the stories of Christmas that bring him the most joy. For example, he could volunteer to dress up as Santa for the local children's hospital, fetch holly and ivy to make a wreath for the front door, or ask his mother to dig out her old recipe for plum pudding.
- Understand the boundaries he should set with respect to spending too much time with people who value different aspects of Christmas.

If we now overlay Nick's and Gloria's Constellations, we can see where their visions of Christmas coincide, and where they diverge. While any differences may be sources of tension in their household, they can also offer surprising opportunities for generosity, as Nick and Gloria can see how to better accommodate each other.

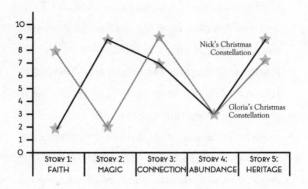

Clearly, Nick and Gloria are in sync in a number of areas, but out of step in a couple of others. Knowing this could spark some interesting conversations, give them a better understanding of each other's point of view, and help them come up with better plans in the future. For example:

- Gloria might not insist on dragging Nick to Midnight Mass this year, as she usually does. Alternatively, Nick might acknowledge that he hadn't appreciated quite how important the religious side of Christmas is to Gloria, and make an extra effort by booking surprise tickets for the candlelit carol service in town.

- Nick might open up about how much he loved Christmas as a child and ask Gloria how he might pass on that magic now, even though they don't have any children of their own. Together, they could come up with a host of ideas, and Nick could finally start to write the first draft of that children's book about Santa's sleigh running out of magic dust while flying over Scotland.

- Having realized that connection is very important to both of them, they might decide to host a Christmas drinks evening for a small group of close friends for the first time in years.

- They might have an honest conversation about money and gifts once they realize that neither of them is too concerned about receiving presents. For instance, they could decide to limit themselves to just one gift each, and promise to choose it (or make it) with love and care. This will reduce the number of hours they have to spend in busy, noisy shopping malls (which they both detest) and give them more time to enjoy the festive lights at the local Christmas market together (which they both love).

If you will be sharing Christmas with someone this year, imagine how they might rate each of their stories and plot their Constellation. This could be a partner, a child, a relative, or a friend. You could even discuss the five stories with them and ask them the Calm Contemplation questions from Chapter 1. This can lead to some wonderful conversations as you start to see Christmas through their eyes. It will certainly help both of you to understand and accommodate the other's view of Christmas.

CALM CONTEMPLATION: YOUR COMBINED CHRISTMAS CONSTELLATIONS

Once you have overlaid your Christmas Constellation with that of a loved one, take a good look at the chart and answer the following questions:

- What do your combined Christmas Constellations tell you?
- What is surprising about the chart?
- What makes real sense?
- Does the chart suggest focusing on anything in particular? If so, what?
- Does the chart suggest avoiding anything in particular? If so, what?
- What kind of year has it been for each of you, and what do you each need from Christmas as a result? How might you provide that for each other?

CHECKING IN EVERY YEAR

Just as stars wander across the night sky, our Christmas Constellations can change over time. Perhaps a dramatic event shifts our perspective. Perhaps a partner's enthusiasm for a particular aspect of Christmas eventually rubs off on us. Perhaps we start a family, or our children fly the nest, or we become more—or less— cynical with age.

It is worth re-creating your Christmas Constellations each year to see what has changed and help you identify what you want and need from the season at this particular moment in your life. Who knows, it might even become one of your favorite annual rituals.

REIMAGINING CHRISTMAS

It is Christmas in the heart that puts Christmas in the air.
—W. T. Ellis[2]

My childhood Christmases were simple and predictable in the best kind of way. I knew we would go to the forest for the tree and make our own decorations, while Grandma made the Christmas cake. There were off-limits cupboards and squeaking floorboards and rustling paper as presents were squirreled away. There was good cheer, the smell of cigar smoke, friends popping in for hugs and drinks and hot mince pies. Caroling at the local retirement home, at school, at church, in the center of town. Daily chocolate in the Advent calendar. Excited talk in the playground about what Father Christmas might bring. The house cozy and welcoming, with tinsel draped on every picture frame, a garland swirling around the stairs, baubles spinning on the tree. The anticipation of Christmas morning so great that it made my older brother nauseous, as it did my mother when she was young.

My first truly white Christmas was celebrated in Yamagata, Japan, at the age of twenty-two. We night-skied on empty slopes, bathed our homesickness in hot springs, and cooked a mishmash of winter delights.

Later in my twenties, Christmas was more about office parties and working until the last minute before putting on Chris Rea's "Driving Home for Christmas" and heading back to family. It was pining for a boyfriend from my childhood bedroom, wondering if I should have bought a home of my own by then.

In my thirties, there were Christmas Eve phone calls from my new love (and soon-to-be husband), followed by post-Christmas getaways to far-flung places. Then marriage, children, and a whole new world of chaos and delight.

*　*　*

Christmas has been a soundtrack to my life, a marker through the decades, ever-evolving but somehow familiar. The traditions we create in our own homes and with our families become part of our legacies. Our Christmas stories are part of us, and as the authors of those stories, it is up to us to choose how they will unfold.

Remembering past Christmases helps us to recognize potential emotional triggers well in advance, and rediscover sources of joy.

CALM CONTEMPLATION: CHRISTMAS PAST, PRESENT, AND FUTURE

- Make notes on the different kinds of Christmases you have experienced. Start each memory on a new line with "The one when . . ." and keep going until you can't think of any more. Try to be specific, and seek out some healthy, positive memories, even if negative ones surface first. If this exercise brings up too much for you, try going through it with a friend or even seeking professional support.

- Now complete this sentence: "I'd like this year to be the one when . . ."

THOUGHTFUL PLANNING

You know that feeling when you are snapped out of a stressful situation by laughter, a kind gesture, or an unexpected occurrence? That is when you open a door to joy. We are all susceptible to tension over Christmas, but there are many opportunities for joyful moments, too. And you can increase their frequency by committing to less, being prepared, spreading out gatherings, delegating, slowing down, and turning chores into mindful exercises or shared activities.

According to a study by the University of Edinburgh, festive stress amounts to more than a little extra pressure. "Christmas hormones"—a potent mix of cortisol, serotonin, and dopamine—race through our bodies, causing highs and lows but mostly chronic fatigue. As the author of the study wrote, "No other event in the calendar has such a deep impact on our behaviour as the annual event called Christmas."[3]

So, how do we prepare for it without a frenzied rush that leaves us exhausted at the front door on the big day, oversized glass of wine in hand, grinning through gritted teeth, wondering what just happened to December?

Last year, as December rolled on, I noticed a lot of people asking, "So, are you ready for Christmas?" But what does that actually mean? Are they asking about a checklist of things that have been done: food in the fridge, house swept, Nativity costume made, presents wrapped, Christmas movie schedule highlighted? Or could it be more than that? Could it mean having explored what the season means to you and your loved ones, and having set time aside to honor that in whatever way you choose? Could it mean having steeled your heart for the challenging moments ahead, with a calm mind to take it all in? Could it mean having shifted your view of Christmas, to invite a nourishing season and moments of joy? It's worth taking a moment to consider what "readying yourself for Christmas" is going to look like this year.

Thoughtful planning can be a powerful antidote to stress. Before you begin, though, let's establish your overall intention for the season, to make sure you plan for the *right* things.

CALM CONTEMPLATION: SETTING YOUR INTENTION

Answer the following questions to set your intention for this year's Christmas:

- Given the kind of year you have had, what kind of Christmas would be most nourishing and appropriate? A loud, celebratory one? A quiet, restful one? A magical, surprise-filled one? A traditional one? An alternative one? A cozy one? A sunny one? Or something else?
- How do you want to feel at the end of it all? What boundaries do you need to set to help you achieve that?
- Overall, what is your intention for Christmas this year?

WHAT IF . . . ?

Sometimes we rush ahead and make plans on autopilot. Hopefully your Christmas Constellation and intention setting will help you to avoid making that mistake this year. Even so, it is worth taking a moment to ponder some deeper questions, as reflecting on the answers can help to make the season really special.

CALM CONTEMPLATION:
WHAT IF . . . ?

Find a quiet spot and consider the following questions:

- What if you could strip away all obligations and expectations and do whatever you want this Christmas? What would you do? Even if this is unrealistic this year, how might you bring the essence of it into your celebrations?
- What if you knew this would be your last Christmas in your current circumstances, or at this par-

ticular stage of life? Perhaps next year you will have a child, become an empty nester, get married, get divorced, move, have an operation, lose your job, find a new job, start a business, get a dog, or do something you haven't even thought of yet. If something is about to change, what should you treasure about *this* Christmas, and how might this affect your approach to preparing, gathering, and spending?

- What if you knew that this would be your last Christmas with someone you love? Consider how you might make this year extra special.

- What if you knew that this would be *your* last Christmas? What would you joyfully say "yes" to? What would you calmly say "no" to? How would you show those you love what they mean to you?

- What if you knew that you will live to be a hundred? How many Christmases would you have left? How might this knowledge help you ease the pressure or make a particular sacrifice this year?

SHARED TIME

My older brother and I are shoveling ourselves into our heavy winter coats, small hands searching for the mittens dangling by elastic from the sleeves. We tumble into the back of the old brown Volvo with our Labrador, Meg, and as soon as Mum has tucked our baby brother into the basket on her knee, we're off.

At first we are loud and fidgety, telling jokes and poking each other in our excitement. "Can we get the tallest one?" we beg in unison, squeezing our faces between the front seats.

"We'll see," my parents say, noncommittal but smiling.

After a while, the voices fall away as the hum of the engine lulls us into our respective dreams of Christmas. I trace the shapes of pine trees in the condensation on the window, clearing the glass one finger-swipe at a time to see the town rushing past, making way for villages, then woodland. As we get closer to Ashurst, we're on the lookout for the hand-painted sign: CHRISTMAS TREES THIS WAY, above a giant arrow pointing to the woods.

"There it is. There it is."

The trees come in all shapes and sizes. I like the fat ones

with lots of room for decorations. Dad suggests getting one a couple of feet taller than our ceiling, so when we cut off the single spindly branch at the top we'll be left with a fine, plump specimen.

Once the tree has been secured on top of the car, we head back. In the past we have stopped off at a forest pub for a bowl of soup and some chips by the fire, but today we are hurrying home, eager to get the tree indoors so Christmas can begin.

Moments like these make Christmas precious. That's not just some warm and fuzzy notion; it's scientific fact. A study in the *BMJ* (formerly the *British Medical Journal*) identified a particular network in the brain that is activated by images associated with Christmas. According to the team from the University of Copenhagen who conducted the research, "The network showed a series of cerebral regions that are more active in people who celebrate Christmas with positive associations compared with people with no Christmas traditions [or] neutral associations."[4] So we are actually hardwired to enjoy Christmas.

I think this is what we mean when we use the word "Christmassy" in relation to our anticipation of Christmas. I'm pretty sure I have never used that word when I'm right in the middle of it, tucking into my roast dinner. It's more subtle than that—the promise of festivities sensed in the air, registered in our brains, held in our hearts. It's a fluttery sensation that arrives quietly, often during a special moment of shared time.

Creating a simple ritual to mark the threshold between work and the holidays can be deeply rewarding. Last year, after a frenetic period of school-related festive activities, we opted for something easy. On the last day of term we took the girls for a blustery walk by the sea after school, and shared our excitement over hot chocolate with tiny marshmallows. That night, we lit a candle and welcomed our family Christmas. It was a simple but special observance that may, with repetition, become a treasured ritual.

Simplicity, generosity, delight, and belonging are the true touchstones of festive joy.

Sometimes, the most precious moments are unexpected, as Hannah Ross shared with me:

When we adopted our daughter, she arrived home just a few days before Christmas. Her world had been turned upside down, so it was an emotional time. On December 23, we went to a local Korean restaurant. While we waited for the food, she started to cry for her Korean foster mother, so I picked her up and walked back and forth with her as she cried into my neck. She was wearing this cute purple outfit with lambs on it. It snowed that year, and we went for a walk and she kissed me in the snow.

This year, amid your preparations, take a moment to dwell in nostalgia for the past, savor delight in the present, and nourish hope for the future.

SHARING THE LOAD

My mum is a master at turning jobs into games, and Christmas is no exception. As a primary school teacher and avid

Christmas-card sender, she usually receives in excess of two hundred cards herself. We help her string them up on red ribbons, then hold a competition to guess how many there are before rushing around to count them. We wear Santa hats and red coats to hand-deliver cards to our neighbors, then claim payment in gingerbread stars.

She involves us in the kitchen too, stirring and rolling and icing, all for the opportunity to lick the spoon.

These days I encourage my own children to participate in all the Christmas preparations. One year, staying in a rented house, we weren't allowed to affix anything to the wall. So, instead of our usual Advent calendar, we made a pile of tiny envelopes into which we popped sweet treats, secret messages, and other fun things. The girls wrote numbers on them and we put them all in a large wooden bowl with a tangle of fairy lights.

We lit candles every night and the girls took turns blowing them out at the end of each meal. We swapped out their autumnal storybooks for festive wintery tales, and spun yarns while making a wreath for the front door.

Sharing time together, and sharing the load, generates many precious moments at this time of year.

MONEY AND SHOPPING

There is something very special about the way cities come to life each December. According to food writer Tom Parker Bowles, a highlight of Christmas in London in the seventeenth and eighteenth centuries was the Frost Fair, held on the frozen Thames. As the medieval bridges were closely packed together, blocks of ice would get lodged between the piers, which encouraged the whole river to freeze. According to Parker Bowles:

> The first recorded Fair was in 1607/8, when the ice was not only thick enough for people to wander and skid from Southwark to the City, but sturdy enough to support football pitches, horse and coach races, fruit sellers, street vendors and the odd pub or two. Shopkeepers burned fires in their tents on the ice, and all London plied its trade.[5]

Festive window displays generously offer inspiration. But when you strip away the decorations, the lights, and the music, the ultimate aim is to part you from your money. An estimated nine out of ten people wake up with a debt hangover each January,[6] while nearly 60 percent of households say they make sacrifices to buy Christmas presents.[7]

There is a similar story on the other side of the Atlantic. Back in 1988, an article in the *Washington Post* was titled "Christmas Run Amok: Our Gift-Giving Has Gotten Out of Hand."[8] More than thirty years on, the annual bill for Christmas shopping in the United States is around $1 trillion.[9]

"Money Saving Expert" Martin Lewis encourages people to stop buying gifts for *anyone* outside their immediate family. He recently lamented:

> Many people feel obliged to buy gifts for others that they know they won't use with money they don't have, and cause themselves stress they don't need . . . It is time for us to get off this gift-giving treadmill. I think sometimes the best gift is releasing others from the obligation of having to give to you . . . Less pressure, less cost, less debt . . . more joy.[10]

By releasing yourself from all of those unnecessary gift-giving obligations—to distant relatives, children of friends, and everyone in your office, for example—you do your bank account a big favor and give a priceless gift to a large group of people who no longer feel obliged to buy for you.

And it's not just the gifts. We also spend vast amounts of money on decorations, food, and travel, much of which we don't even categorize as Christmas spending.

Although it is hard to escape retail pressure, there are things we can do. I received a post-Christmas sale notice in my inbox on December 17 last year, which prompted me to unsubscribe from nearly every promotional email.

I'm not saying we shouldn't buy *anything*. I love a Christmas market or street strung with Christmas lights as much as the next person, but let's not be naive to the manipulation. We must choose what we want to experience, buy, give, or simply leave on the shelf.

Personally, I cringe every time a news headline announces with great solemnity that another retail giant has suffered a slight decline in sales growth (which means its sales are still growing, albeit not quite as fast as they were last year). Who decided it's a bad thing that more of us are buying from independent shops, handmade gifts, making presents ourselves, or simply spending less than we once did? Who said we shouldn't focus on our mental health and keep our stress levels low by buying at small, local independent shops or online instead of jostling with other irate shoppers in noisy, airless shopping malls?

This year, impose some boundaries on your shopping and spending and see the difference it makes to your well-being.

HOW TO SPEND LESS THIS CHRISTMAS

If you want to reduce your Christmas spending, drafting a budget is essential. There is something about the word "budget" that makes many of us shudder. Perhaps it sounds miserly or restrictive? This year, try to think of it in a different way—as a voluntary constraint that will allow your creativity to flourish, and help you to do what you love.

Use the following prompts to help manage your spending:

1. Before looking ahead to work out a budget for this year, look back at last year and calculate what you spent. This might be painful, but it is essential, and ultimately it can be motivating. Get out your old bank and credit card statements and estimate what you spent on:

- gifts for immediate family and very close friends
- gifts for your wider social circle (distant relatives, work colleagues, teachers, Secret Santa, etc.)
- Christmas cards and postage
- food (for every gathering you hosted, not just Christmas Day, including any food you prepared ahead of time)
- decorations (including the tree and lights, obviously, but also any new furniture you bought, such as extra chairs for the dining table)
- wrapping paper, ribbon, and tape
- new clothes and shoes
- makeup, hair appointments, and other beauty treats

- socializing (festive meals and drinks, tickets for concerts, cash withdrawals, etc.)
- superfluous "because it's Christmas" purchases
- travel (including accommodations, train and plane tickets, fuel, parking fees, etc.)
- donations to charity
- tips to babysitters, hairdressers, manicurists, doormen, etc.
- anything else specifically related to Christmas.

Now add it all up. You'll probably be shocked, but that's okay.

2. If someone gave you that amount of money right now, no strings attached, what difference would it make in your life, or in the life of someone you love? What experiences might you try? What dreams would you pursue? What support could you offer someone else?

3. With this in mind, channel any regret or frustration into a commitment to spend wisely this year. Decide on a figure that you are happy to spend—one that will not leave you feeling stressed or overextended. Write it down. If you feel unable to pluck a number out of thin air, calculate 0.5–1.2 percent of your annual

income. This will give you a rough idea of the average cost of Christmas for people in your income bracket.[11] Of course, you are not obliged to spend that, but it can be a useful guide.

4. Reduce the figure you have calculated by 10 percent, in anticipation of a budget overrun, which often happens.

5. Now comes the fun part. Work out how you are going to create a mindful, meaningful, and memorable Christmas within your budget. If you start with what you are willing to spend, rather than buy first and add up later, you will feel much better come January.

6. Calculate what you expect to save compared to last year, then translate that into something that would mean a lot to you or someone else. For example, if you can spend 30 percent less than you did last year, you could finally enroll in that creative writing course you have been longing to take, pay off a chunk of debt, or start a savings account for a young relative. Either note down your goal or create an image that represents how you'll feel when you have achieved it, then put the slip of paper in your purse or wallet. Whenever you are tempted to buy something unnecessary, it will

Ten Ways to Reduce Spending at Christmas

1. Create a budget.

2. Call a halt to unnecessary gift-giving. Buy for fewer people, and less for everyone. You'll be surprised how many people are grateful that they don't have to buy you something in return.

3. Consider what you might give—your time, skills, creativity, or attention—in place of merchandise (see Chapter 4).

4. Write down gift ideas for the people who are still on your list. As you buy or make their presents, check them off so you don't double up. When you are looking for specific gifts, shop around and take advantage of seasonal bargains, but don't get sucked into buying anything you don't need just because it's on sale.

5. Simplify your gatherings. Hold winter picnics rather than lavish dinners, or invite guests to contribute something (see Chapter 5).

6. If possible, don't buy on credit, unless you can pay

it off immediately. Instead, use Christmas funds that you have built up over the year. It feels more real that way, and you avoid the debt hangover.

7. Avoid expensive annual rituals, such as taking the whole family to the ballet, unless those events are a true source of joy.

8. When you are ready to wrap, spread out all the presents on a table or the floor and check what you have bought or made for each person. Now assess each gift. If you realize the gift is not right, return the item for a refund.

9. Stay offline as much as possible. There were 34 percent more online shopping searches on Christmas Day than Black Friday in 2016,[12] and retailers don't take a break from aggressive marketing over the holidays.

10. If you have a partner or children, discuss your plans with them.

be right there to remind you precisely why you are being more careful this year.

7. If difficult feelings about money arise, acknowledge them, but then return to your Constellation and your budget to remind yourself why you are doing things differently.

8. Whenever you go shopping, compile a list and stick to it, compare prices, and try not to get distracted. When you are tempted to buy something, pause for a moment and ask yourself if it supports your intention for Christmas this year. When shopping online, leave the items in your cart for a while before checking out. Ensure that all of your purchases are mindful (see Chapter 4) and that your spending correlates with your Constellation.

9. Keep a record as you shop, and celebrate when you stay within your budget.

CLAIMING CHRISTMAS

It takes confidence and courage to make changes to something that has been done the same way for years or even decades. But I urge you to take the plunge for the sake of all your future Christmases.

By now, I hope you are starting to feel calmer about the onset of Christmas, and less overwhelmed by the prospect of planning, spending, and gift-giving. But this, in itself, is not enough to ensure a truly calm Christmas and a season of festive joy.

Before everything else,
we must take care of ourselves.

Without a strong foundation of nourishment, rest, and self-care, even the most meticulously laid plans will soon unravel. So, in the next chapter, we step away from planning and into the natural flow of the season as we explore comfort and joy in the depths of winter.

CHAPTER 3

Comfort and Joy in Winter

DEER AT DAWN

"It's time to go," my father whispers around my bedroom door, the hall light falling in a strip on the soft gray carpet. "Are you coming?"

Within ten minutes, I am wide awake, dressed and downstairs, slathering Marmite onto toast, as Dad warms up the car. His bag is sitting on the table, holding his camera and lenses, black-and-white film, and hope for some special sightings. We are about to embark on a dawn raid of the New Forest, in search of deer.

It is thrilling to know the rest of the family—and most of the country—is still asleep. The only light outside is the dull orange of the streetlights.

A milky mist hangs low. It is cold and damp in the forest this morning, and frosty leaf litter crunches beneath my feet.

"Shhh, try to stay quiet," says Dad in his booming whisper. "They are nearby."

Then, out from between two holly bushes, steps a fallow fawn. She does a double take when she sees us, then steadies herself and stares. I wonder if the white markings on her brown back are snow. One ear twitches, listening for her mother, but her eyes remain focused on us. On me. She is trying to tell me something, and I am quick to trust her. She stays there a full minute, singing softly with her huge brown eyes, making an intense connection with my young mind. Then she turns and skitters off.

Years later, reading about spirit animals, I learn that the deer symbolizes tenderness tempered with strength. It is often seen as a symbol of the heart chakra—compassionate and gentle—and an image of love. In addition, its ability to grow a new set of antlers each year has made it a powerful symbol of regeneration and renewal.

Today, more than three decades later, as I stand once more on frosty ground at the edge of winter, I call on my nine-year-old self and her deer to lend us their secret, so I may approach the festive season with tenderness tempered with strength. Let's carry the spirit of the deer with us into December, offer compassion and love over Christmas, and invite gentle renewal for the year to come.

WINTER RHYTHMS

For us children, winter is getting dressed between the storage heater and the ring of drying clothes, trying not to burn our behinds as we balance on one leg to pull on our school socks. It is Advent candles at Sunday school, afternoon baths, and indoor picnics. It is baking, carol singing, hot soup, casseroles, and bedtime stories. Pressing noses against the window of the big toy shop in town, dreaming of what Santa might bring.

It is gloopy porridge on Monday mornings. Reluctant car engines, warm water poured over the windscreen, and the laborious scraping of ice. A garden left to its own devices, the treehouse ivy-covered and lonely. Wellies for splashing through puddles and see-through umbrellas. Hot-water bottles and extra blankets and not being allowed outside with wet hair. Grandma polishing the brass candlesticks and making deep-crust pies. Mum filling the cupboards and knowing that we will be fine if we are snowed in . . . which never happens. The humdrum of daily life, drumming like the rain on the roof.

This was the rhythm of my childhood winters. The simple things that centered us while December swirled around our tiny shoulders.

These days, like a heavy boot on a frozen puddle, December cracks me wide open as it closes in. It makes me worry about the farmers and the pigs, and the shepherds and the sheep, battling the cold and the rain. The homeless people tucked into doorways and under bridges, the elderly sitting alone at their breakfast tables, hoping someone might pop in. The early risers in their dressing gowns, carrying their worries into the kitchen to put the kettle on and figure out how to pay for Christmas.

The sounds of winter are crackling poetry. Wind in the trees. Rain on the roof. A spitting fire. The thump of a log falling away from the flames. Rustling paper. Mulled wine poured steaming into a glass. The rhythm of the weather forecast calmly announcing that the storms will rage on.

Joy and sorrow go together in winter like the play of

light and shadow in the flicker of a candle. Every one of us will experience a full range of emotions before spring returns.

> *Joy and sorrow hover in the margins*
> *of our winter days.*

I have long wondered whether the January blues might be due to more than the miserable weather, the monotony of the return to work, the short, gray days and the long, dark nights. What if it is also a consequence of the way we spend December? What if the typical sluggishness, lack of motivation, and low mood are hangovers from the festive stress, an excess of rich food, and the disruption of our usual daily rhythms when Christmas descends? Imagine the difference it would make if we could usher ourselves through the month with care and allow plenty of time for rest and reflection.

It is important to nourish body, mind, and spirit, seek out small moments of joy, and establish comforting winter rhythms that will see you right through the season. There is a restorative power in winter, an invitation to slow down and harness that intangible, special something that lives in the corridors of Christmas. It can be a hectic time, but with a little mindfulness and the occasional pause, it can also offer countless opportunities for rejuvenation and joy.

FINDING YOUR NATURAL RHYTHM IN WINTER

When we surrender to the flow of winter, a powerful wave carries us far from the rush of everyday life and inwards, to the place where our truth lies waiting. This is a time to reconnect with our essence, our humanity, our deep-seated creativity, and our place in nature.

Much of what has come to represent Christmas in the twenty-first century—bright lights, crowded shopping malls, aggressive online sales, rowdy office parties, long to-do lists, and a heavy burden of social obligations— is characterized by frenetic energy and noise levels that run counter to our natural tendency to hibernate, retreat into ourselves, and rest at this time of year.

Industrial advances have pushed us far out of alignment with our natural rhythms. We extend the day with electric lighting that is exponentially brighter than the candlelight that eased our forefathers into a midwinter evening, or the weak sunlight that gently nudged them awake. As we addictively check phones and work on laptops late into the night, we set our brains racing at the very moment when we should be settling down to sleep. If we never switch off our devices, it's hard to switch off our minds for long enough to inhabit the here and now, or to fall into a deep, restful sleep.

The choices we make in the first couple weeks of December can affect the way we experience the whole season, and how we emerge into the New Year, so let's choose well.

LEARNING FROM NATURE

Winter is hoarfrost on the hedgerow, crunchy leaves on the ground, seasoned wood for chopping, bare trees silhouetted against a stark sky. But if you look closely, there is still color . . . and even a little industry.

According to Charlie Mellor of the Woodland Trust, hibernating animals such as hedgehogs don't check out completely when they cozy up for the winter.[1] After nourishing themselves throughout the autumn to build up their fat reserves, they slow their heart rate and breathing, lower their temperature, and reduce their metabolism to use up as little of those vital stores of energy as possible. They can survive for long periods without eating anything at all, but they still get up from time to time to snuffle for a little extra nutrition or to relieve themselves away from their nests.

Hedgehogs have the right idea. They know that resting over winter does not mean ditching every plan and routine, taking three months off, and lounging in bed all day. Instead, they merely cut down on their usual feverish activity and focus on the essentials. For us, this equates to taking time for the simple things that will keep us feeling good all the way to spring—cooking healthy meals, going for bracing walks, moisturizing dry skin, journaling thoughts about the year gone past, cozying up with a book, or catching up with friends. This is a time to seek out moments of pleasure that are even more gratifying against the gray backdrop of the season.

The work of winter is focused on taking care of what is already there, protecting and preparing. In the home, it's a time to mend and maintain—checking the boiler, clearing gutters, fixing leaks, insulating pipes. In gardens, it's a time for pruning fruit trees, protecting plants from frosts, building up the compost heap, and digging over the plot. But there's also nothing wrong with spending a bitter December afternoon curled up in an armchair flicking through seed catalogues and making choices for the spring. At this time of year it's natural to slow down, prune our lives of extraneous details, reflect on past events, and tend our hearts, minds, and bodies so we are ready to flourish again.

> *Winter is surprisingly kind in many ways,*
> *but mostly because it expects so little of us.*

The day is still dark but the birds are awake, and I wonder if there is anything quite like the luxury of sitting up in bed with hot tea and toast, reading poetry, a thick patchwork blanket around your shoulders.

Later, I am tramping between fields in my wellies and I wonder if there is anything quite like the luxury of a country lane to yourself on a clear winter's day.

Then I meet up with a friend for coffee. We huddle in the corner of the café, talking about Christmas plans, and how our children have grown, and the books that make us feel better when it rains all day. And I wonder, for a moment, if there is anything quite like the luxury of a friend and a coffee shop and a chat about books.

Then the door flies open and my husband and the girls tumble in, buttoned up warm and freshly whipped by the wind, and I am smothered in kisses and small people hanging from my neck. And I know there is no greater luxury than love.

CALM CONTEMPLATION:
WINTER RHYTHMS

Sit somewhere quiet and ponder these questions:

- What brings you comfort at this time of year?
- What brings you joy?
- What would radical winter wellness look like for you?

NOURISH YOUR MIND

Walking in winter is different. Cold air splashes your face and your breath is visible in the air. Everything crunches underfoot. You sense the beginning of a slip on a patch of ice, then feel the correction that comes with a quick in-breath as you steady yourself. The trees are vulnerable in their nakedness, their branches cleared for robins and other feathered friends to meet and natter. The freezing air traces its way all the way to your lungs, snapping you into the present and giving you a sense of vitality.

97

The skies are different in winter too, and I love to linger by the seashore and watch them. I live on the Jurassic Coast, near a town famous for fossils, which are revealed at the bottom of the cliffs like tiny gifts after every storm, disclosing their 180-million-year-old secrets to anyone with a hammer and some patience. An ancient town that was featured in the Domesday Book, it has a bustling harbor, and the best fish and chips for miles around. I love to order grilled sea bass from the tiny hut known as The Fisherman's Wife, and lick my salty fingers in the slashing rain as I shelter by the lifeboat, laughing as my four-year-old insists on splashing in the puddles instead of taking cover.

This is my kind of late-November moment, a welcome alternative to the shopping malls and online hustle that begins with Black Friday and continues right up to Christmas. Shopping for that special gift can be a delight if you are in the right frame of mind, especially when you start early and aren't in a hurry, but the constant call of sales can be really stressful. Taking regular breaks from the high street, and the promotions in your inbox, can do wonders to keep you calm in the run-up to Christmas.

Nourishing your mind can be as simple as turning away from overstimulation—to-do lists, screens, loud music, bright lights, toxic conversations—and making your way into nature, open spaces, fresh air, peace and quiet. Try counting the shades of evergreens, inhaling the aroma of wild herbs, listening for signs of life. On cold, sunny days, look for berries, or different leaf shapes, or visiting birds. Seek out hardy plants emerging from cracks in the pavement. Make bark rubbings with a little person. Fill up a feeder for the birds.

I find the ever-changing sky a powerful tonic for the soul. For you, it might be the nearness of water, or the bare bones of trees, stripped of their leaves. Seek whatever you need. Document your finds. Photograph them. Sketch them. Forage a few samples for your bedside table.

Or nourish your mind with words—write about your day, take time out with an inspiring podcast or a good book, or settle in for a long conversation.

IN THE BLEAK MIDWINTER

Winters in the northern hemisphere can be harsh. Although there have only been ten "white" Christmases in England over the past century,[2] I still associate Christmas with snow. In reality, though, we are more likely to get wind and rain along with the short days and dark afternoons.

Many of us feel low from time to time in this season, but it can be much more serious for those who suffer from Seasonal Affective Disorder (SAD). Twenty-nine percent of adults experience some symptoms of SAD, such as low energy levels, lack of self-esteem, and anxiety, and 8 percent of people suffer from an acute form of the condition.[3]

A groundbreaking study in 2016 revealed that light therapy—either on its own or in combination with antidepressants—is not only effective but superior to treatment with antidepressants alone. Taking midwinter trips, spending time outdoors, and exercise can be effective antidotes to SAD.

In the UK, the National Health Service also advocates a series of lifestyle changes—such as getting as much natural sunlight as possible, exercising regularly, and managing your stress levels—to alleviate the symptoms of SAD.[4] Sufferers add that oily fish (or omega-3 supplements) and vitamin D can work wonders as well.[5] It is worth consulting a nutritionist for tailored dietary advice.

SIMPLIFY YOUR LIFE

Over the years, I have discovered that simplicity is the key to a calm winter. Simplifying "out there"—your spaces and schedules—can usher in order and quietude. Meanwhile, simplifying "in here"—through presence and mindfulness—can foster deep tranquility.

If possible, bend and shape your workload so you are not buried under a mound of tasks at a time when your body just wants to rest. If you work shifts, or in an industry like retail or hospitality that ramps up as Christmas approaches, take extra care to schedule downtime and nourish yourself with good food, plenty of hydration, and lots of sleep.

Guard against overcommitment. Don't accept every invitation; give yourself a few nights off each week. If you have children, consider reducing their after-school activities and use the time to do more things together at home.

Think ahead. November and December weekends and evenings are the perfect times to prepare for the season in a way that feels joyful and enriching, not stressful and draining. Make your own fruit preserves, or go for an early evening forage and create some natural decorations from what you find. Fashion an Advent calendar full of daily reminders and little treats that will keep you connected to your own well-being as the season progresses.

Christmas is not a single day; it is a season, and a manifestation of the spirit of generosity. It's a time for cherishing loved ones and using our skills and talents to create moments and memories. But it also takes place in the middle of winter, so we must be careful not to overextend ourselves. It's vital that we take some time to rest and reflect, and cherish ourselves, too.

Approached in a gentle way, Christmas can be a time of nourishment and rejuvenation as you bask in the glow of friendship and thoughtfulness, both bestowed and received. Grant yourself special moments every now and again to tune in to the season and soak up the atmosphere of goodwill.

NOURISH YOUR BODY

Delicious, healthy food doesn't have to be complicated. Roast a chicken with garlic, lemon, and thyme, slow-cook a soul-warming stew, rustle up a parsley risotto, simmer a cauliflower curry, pop a casserole in the oven and some greens in a steamer. Bone broth is good for the soul as well as the body.

Brassicas like cabbages, cauliflowers, Brussels sprouts, and kale are in full flush in midwinter, flaunting their thick green leaves and demanding inclusion in substantial soups. Root vegetables like turnips, parsnips, and celeriac are abundant, too, as are winter salads. You might find endive, arugula, lettuce, winter citrus for vitamin C, and herbs for your teapot.

Cookbooks are my guilty pleasure. I retreat to them when the wind is whirling around our house or the rain is pelting down, but there are also many great recipes online. Choose ingredients that will boost your immune system, and stock up on warming spices like turmeric, black pepper, and cardamom. Scientists at the University of Prague have found that nutmeg, cinnamon, cloves, and star anise all contain mood-enhancing chemicals, so in one way at least, those delicious Christmas biscuits are actually good for us.[6]

Some friends swear by "golden milk" to boost immunity, help the digestive system, and reduce inflammation. Made with cashew nuts, fresh turmeric root, ginger, cinnamon, and honey, it is full of winter goodness and brings a gentle glow to the skin. I like to stew peeled and chopped apples with cinnamon and orange juice, then add some natural yogurt for a simple breakfast or a sprinkling of crushed gingernuts for a warming dessert.

If Dry January is inspired by a desire to detox, it is bookended by the Christmas "tox" and the February "retox." It really makes no sense to feed ourselves so much alcohol and sugar just when we are at our most bruised and weary after a long year. Surely it would be better for our systems to take it easy all the way through. Maybe indulge occasionally, but keep it light most of the time. Not only will you save money, but you'll likely get a better night's sleep, be in a better mood, have a better complexion, and have more energy to enjoy the special moments.

Sometimes indulgence is a form of escape from current circumstances, but by nourishing yourself throughout the season, you will be better placed to make any fundamental changes in your life that will reduce the need to escape in the first place.

KEEP YOUR ROUTINES

Many of our routines go out the window around Christmastime, but it's crucial to maintain the important ones. For me, that means stretching, eating a good breakfast, writing in my journal, reading with my little ones, watering the house plants, and sipping chamomile tea before bed. Routines help keep children grounded, and give you a sense of stability throughout the day.

Try to keep moving. If you attend a yoga class, keep

it up. If not, try dancing around the kitchen while you're making breakfast. Or wrap up warm and go for a long walk, run, or bike ride. There will be many times when exercising might seem like the last thing you want to do, but just tell yourself that you are sure to feel the benefit afterwards. Let the fresh winter air revitalize your body, mind, and spirit.

After a long stint at my desk, I often notice my feet are cold. It helps to put a few drops of eucalyptus oil on a wet facecloth in the shower and hop in for a cleansing steam. A luxuriant bath can also go a long way to warming your bones, soothing aching muscles, and helping you to relax after a tiring commute or a busy day. I use a combination of Epsom salts, lemongrass, and rosemary from a local apothecary for a restorative soak. And moisturizing afterwards is a lovely, nourishing ritual.

NOURISH YOUR SPIRIT

Go gently into each winter morning. On waking, set aside a moment to check in with yourself, greet the day, take a deep breath, and smile. Tiptoe into the kitchen. Light a candle. Meditate or write in your journal. Putter around in the half-light. Stretch. Listen to some calming music. Put on your wellies and step outside. Give yourself the gift of a winter sunrise. Take good care of yourself.

CALM CONTEMPLATION:
SIMPLIFY AND NOURISH

- How could you simplify your home?
- How could you simplify your schedule?
- How could you simplify your digital life?
- How else could you nourish your mind?
- How else could you nourish your body?
- How else could you nourish your spirit?
- How else could you nourish your loved ones?
- How could you prepare yourself better for sleep?
- What rituals could you create to see you through winter?

PART 2

Celebration:
During Christmas

CHAPTER 4

Mindful Gifting

MINDFUL GIFTING

In the library of my mind, I hold many images of Christmases past. There's a young girl at a Christmas fair, eking out her pocket money to buy gifts for her family. On the next page the same girl is huddled at the desk in her bedroom, hand-stamping Christmas cards. Then she is opening the first door on her Advent calendar on December 1, a hint of Christmas magic encircling her.

The girl and her brothers are opening their stockings by the light of the landing, each reaching in to find a bag of chocolate coins, a clementine, and a silver dollar tucked into the toe.

Only a handful of my memories are directly related to what was contained inside wrapped packages on Christmas Day. Instead, it is the anticipation of those gifts that features most prominently, and the fun of giving and receiving. I can't actually remember what was left under the tree for most years. I wish I had reminded myself of this before embarking on the journey that is "Christmas with Children."

As I have mentioned, our elder daughter was born on Christmas Day. One year later, on her first birthday, she snuggled into bed with us first thing in the morning and opened the tiny stocking that held her first-ever Christmas gift—a little white rabbit. She kept looking to each of us, then back to the rabbit, as if she couldn't quite believe it was for her. It was so precious, but sadly thereafter, her wonder faded with each additional gift, of which there were far too many.

As it was her first birthday and Christmas combined, our family and friends went overboard and our large tree was swamped by a deluge of gifts. It took all day to open them, and we were left knee-deep in wrapping paper and pink plastic presents, feeling an odd mix of gratitude and nausea.

After that, we knew something had to change. So first we asked the family for no more plastic gifts, and they kindly obliged. Then Mr. K and I decided to stop exchanging gifts with our siblings and contribute to a kitty to buy one present for each niece or nephew. These days there is less pressure, less waste, and less regret, and the children really appreciate the gift they are given.

> *Mindful gifting comes down to three questions: whether to give, what to give, and how to give.*

WHETHER TO GIVE

Gifting is part of the fabric of human relationships in every culture on earth. And make no mistake, it is a social contract. You give to me, I accept the gift, then I am obliged to reciprocate by giving you something of equivalent value. Anthropologists say the only exception is gift-giving between parents and children, when parents obviously tend to spend more while their children are young.[1]

This cultural waltz is so powerful that it causes annual stress and drives us to the cash registers in droves.

The simplest way to deal with it, and reduce unnecessary spending and waste, is to release as many people as possible from this social contract by not buying them anything. If you have always exchanged gifts with someone, you may need to have a slightly awkward conversation so they don't invoke the contract once again this year. But if you talk it through with them, they should soon understand that this could be the most generous gift you can give each other.

In *The Book of Joy*, an account of a weeklong conversation between Archbishop Desmond Tutu and the Dalai Lama, the two wise elders identify and then whittle down eight "pillars of joy": "Four [of the pillars] were qualities of the mind: *perspective, humility, humor, and acceptance*. Four were qualities of the heart: *forgiveness, gratitude, compassion, and generosity*. . . . We would end up, ultimately, at compassion and generosity. . . ."[2] I believe that mindful gift-giving is supported by both of these "pillars." It is with compassion that we consider the recipient's preferences, current circumstances, and needs; and it is with generosity that we sacrifice something—be it money, time, or energy—to present the gift to them. Compassion without generosity is pity, rather than gifting. Generosity without compassion—buying without considering the burden of a return obligation—is not really generous at all.

> *When we give with genuine generosity*
> *and compassion, we generate joy*
> *for the recipient and ourselves.*

WHAT TO GIVE

These days, with so much access to credit, if we want something, we buy it. Indeed, we can usually have it in our hands within twenty-four hours, our lust almost immediately sated. This is convenient, and it has given us far more choice than our parents and grandparents ever had, but it has also erased the thrill of delayed gratification, and made it surprisingly difficult to choose gifts that people really want or need. Nevertheless, we keep on spending and giving, and the landfills keep on growing.

One report suggested that sixty million unwanted

115

gifts were given in 2018 in the UK alone.[3] That is probably a conservative estimate. A survey found that six out of every ten presents gifted to a sample of two thousand adults were unwanted.[4] Given that so many of us are stretching our finances and stressing about buying these presents, this seems an outrageous waste of money, a glaring environmental problem, and a wholly unnecessary burden on our collective mental health.

Economists have a name for the difference between what we know we have actually spent on someone else and what they perceive we have spent on them: the "deadweight loss." According to a notable paper on the topic in the *American Economic Review*:

> An important feature of gift-giving is that consumption choices are made by someone other than the final consumer. A potentially important microeconomic aspect of gift-giving is that gifts may be mismatched with the recipients' preferences. In the standard microeconomic framework of consumer choice, the best a gift-giver can do with, say, $10 is to duplicate the choice that the recipient would have made. While it is possible for a giver to choose

a gift which the recipient ultimately values above its price—for example, if the recipient is not perfectly informed—it is more likely that the gift will leave the recipient worse off than if she had made her own consumption choice with an equal amount of cash. In short, gift-giving is a potential source of deadweight loss.[5]

The study suggests that holiday gift-giving destroys between 10 percent and one-third of the value of all gifts, depending on who does the giving. By this reckoning, at least $70 billion is wasted in the United States alone every Christmas through this "deadweight loss."[6]

Just imagine the benefits to our wallets, well-being, and the world if we were to eliminate any unnecessary, wasteful gifting, and instead focus on a few mindful gifts for those who really matter to us.

THE ART OF GIFTING

Every year, I see people filling bags and baskets with special offers in the run-up to Christmas, muttering,

"That'll do for so-and-so." But we all know that the likelihood of that person's ideal gift somehow coinciding with the latest three-for-two offer at the supermarket is minutely low. If you choose any old bargain as a gift for someone, it begs the question whether you should be buying them a Christmas present at all.

Take a moment to think about each friend or relative you *really* want to offer a gift to this year. Ask what they need right now. Maybe discuss it with them well ahead of time. It'll be fun and they'll be touched by your thoughtfulness. Pick their brains with probing questions such as, "What's your secret dream?" "What's holding you back?" or "What are you curious about?" This can help you to choose a meaningful gift, and your present will remind them that you really listened to what they had to say.

Here are my three gifting guideposts to help you decide what, if anything, to give to someone.

Gifting Guideposts

Before you choose a gift, ask yourself:

1. Is it mindful?
2. Is it meaningful?
3. Is it memorable?

IS IT MINDFUL?

A mindful gift shows you have been paying attention. For example, we were grateful when our friends and family respected our request not to give plastic presents to our children.

My friend Mandy Gentleman, who lost her beloved mother five years ago, received a particularly thoughtful gift from her mum's best friend last Christmas:

Betty gave me a box filled with dozens of photos of Mum that I had never seen. Memories that made

119

me feel closer than ever to her on a day I find truly tough. Tears fell down my face, but they were tears of happiness, partly because of the pictures, but also knowing how much Betty must care for me to take the time to dig out all the photos. It was one of the best presents I've ever been given.

Before you buy any gift, ask yourself the following questions:

- Is it mindful of what they have experienced this year?
- Is it appropriate given the current context of their life?
- Is it appropriate given their view of the environment and the world?
- Is it appropriate given their thoughts about parenting?
- Is it in line with their attitude to gifts in general?
- Is it in line with what you can afford?
- Is it in line with what they can afford to give in return (so you don't skew the social gifting contract)?

There's no need to answer "yes" to every one of these questions, but if the majority of your answers are "no," it's probably worth thinking again.

IS IT MEANINGFUL?

Meaningful gifts have an extra layer of value. For example, my younger brother handcrafted the mantelpiece for our home, and my dad promised to plant hanging baskets that would give us blooming flowers all summer long.

The following questions can help you choose a truly meaningful gift:

- Is it linked to something they care about, rather than something you care about?
- Does it strengthen the bond between the two of you?
- Does it recognize their gifts and talents . . . and encourage them?
- Does it represent some aspect of your relationship?

- Does it enhance their life in some way?
- Does it offer shared time with someone they care about?
- Is it obviously personal to them?

IS IT MEMORABLE?

Finally, will the recipient remember your gift? Will it live on in their mind and heart long into the future? For example, my older brother once sponsored a chair in my favorite café where I would often go to work. He had a brass plaque with a humorous, personal message screwed into the back of it. I didn't own the chair or take it home with me, but I thought about my brother every time I sat in it, and his donation supported a small business I cared about.

Sarah Alden, mother of two teenagers, came up with another inspirational idea:

This year I gave my children a box called "The Gift of Time," with twelve envelopes in it. On the first of every month they open one of the cards and it tells them what we are going to do together. We put it in the diary and make it happen, then write about our adventures in a scrapbook to leaf through at the end of the year.

The following questions can help you choose a memorable gift:

- Is there something about it that makes it different from any old item grabbed off the shelf at the last moment?
- Does the gift itself or the way you present it surprise and delight in some way?
- Does it remind the recipient of a precious experience, time, or place?
- Will they treasure it?
- Does it allow the recipient to build value through their use or consumption of it (such as a skills development course or a sewing machine that will help them launch a homewares business)?

WRAPPING WITH CARE

An anthropological study of gift-giving in the United States concluded that we wrap presents to transform them from impersonal commodities into sentimental gifts.[7] The study suggested that homemade gifts—and particularly food gifts—are less likely to be extravagantly wrapped because they are already deeply personal by virtue of being made by hand. So, could it be that the wrapping is just as important as the gift itself? If that is the case, we could probably spend a lot less on gifts as long as we take a little extra care wrapping them.

As a teenager, my dream Saturday job was wrapping presents at one of the glitzy stores on Oxford Street in London. My love of parceling things up has now become part of our family lore, enhanced by many years in Japan, where wrapping has been elevated to an art form.

I must admit that I enjoy wrapping even more than thinking up presents for people. There are just so many possibilities with fabric and paper, ribbons and tags. Each decision is a tiny joy, and the process itself can be deeply therapeutic. Mr. K likes to write cryptic clues on gift labels, while I love nothing more than creating a treasure hunt that leads step-by-step to a hidden present.

Linda Maitland, now in her sixties, told me about a particular childhood Christmas with a smile:

When I was seven I really wanted a bike. I remember opening a box with a note inside that said I had to recite my nine times table. Then another note leading me to a big box that took ages to unwrap. There was a bell in it, with a note saying my parents would be saving bit by bit for a bike. I believed that, but after a few more games I was blindfolded and led into the kitchen, where my new bike was revealed. I screamed with joy. How I loved that bike.

If you don't like wrapping, try turning it into a mindfulness exercise. Focus on the feel and sound of the paper as you cut and fold and stick it, and think about the person who will unwrap the gift.

For all my love of wrapping, I do worry about the environment, and the huge amounts of waste that are created every Christmas. The more we buy and give

Top Tips for Saving Money and Reducing Waste When Wrapping Gifts

- Simply give fewer presents.
- Ask for those you do buy to be shipped with as little packaging as possible, and get multiple items shipped together.
- Reuse paper from last year, and keep paper from this year.
- Avoid sparkly or coated wrapping paper as it cannot be recycled, and most glitter contains microplastics.
- Use fabric and tie the corners *furoshiki* style,[8] or fold it around your gift and tie with a ribbon.
- Wrap on the diagonal. (This saves a surprising amount of paper.)
- Fold and tuck in the sides, using the weight of

the gift. (This saves on sticky tape and makes it easier to reuse the paper.)

- Repurpose old maps, newspaper, or pages from magazines, as well as baskets and tins.
- Use uncoated brown kraft paper as a neutral base. It looks gorgeous with sprigs of greenery and raffia or festive ribbons, or when personalized using paint, stamps, or photographs.
- Use beeswax wraps, as these can be washed and repurposed to wrap food. They are easy to make by coating squares of fabric with melted beeswax.[9]
- Be creative with your stationery: recycle old envelopes and shopping bags and collage onto them with old Christmas cards, tape, or stamps.[10]
- Be generous with your ribbon as this will make it easier for the recipient to reuse it.
- If mailing, reuse packaging material wherever possible.

junk we don't want or need, the more we feed the problem. Being more mindful about what we give, how much we give, and how we give it benefits not only our wallets and stress levels but also the planet. And there are ways to wrap without waste.

SENDING LOVE

Crafting was a huge part of Christmas for me when I was growing up. I adored making my own cards, cotton-wool snow, felt Father Christmases, twilled paper stars. There was deep satisfaction as the products rolled off my personal production line, and I was able to think about each of my friends as I wrote out their names in my bubbly teenage writing.

These days, Christmas cards are declining in popularity, as consumers switch from large packs to individual cards, e-cards, and even social media messages. One 2017 survey suggested that fewer than half of all twenty-five- to thirty-four-year-olds in the UK send any cards at all.[11]

Copywriter Louise Heaps, who spent fourteen years

writing greetings cards for Hallmark,[12] recalled sweltering midsummer planning meetings during which Christmas music was played in an attempt to get into the festive spirit. Ultimately, her job always boiled down to finding words that would help customers communicate understanding, caring, and empathy.

Personally, these days, I send only a handful of Christmas cards to people who have been particularly supportive over the course of the year and those I will not see over the holidays. I buy themed stamps from the post office, set aside an afternoon with a festive drink and some Christmas music, and write brief letters inside each one. It's lovely to feel the flow of ink on paper and let someone know you care. It's also a gentle way to reach out to someone who may be having a hard time: there's no need for them to respond, but they will know they have been in your thoughts.

GIFTING YOURSELF

Finally, what will you give yourself this year?

One friend of mine bought herself a two-day retreat. Yet another gave herself the gift of quitting her job.

What would be a mindful, meaningful, and memorable gift for you? Have you told anyone else about it? If not, perhaps you should get it for yourself.

CALM CONTEMPLATION: MINDFUL GIFTING, MINDFUL RECEIVING

- Who are you going to release from a social gifting contract this year?
- What would truly delight those who do receive a gift from you this Christmas? How will you make their presents mindful, meaningful, and memorable?
- What about you? What do you *really* want for Christmas this year?

CHAPTER 5

Heart and Hearth

HOME SWEET HOME

At Christmastime I most notice the changing shapes of things. We are gathered for Christmas lunch. My grandma is in her favorite over-the-knee tweed skirt and the high-necked powder-blue blouse she saves for best. She's not really with it these days, puttering in the margins of dementia, but she's here today. She moved in next door a few years back, when it got to be too much to live in a big old house up north all by herself.

I'm fourteen, still learning to navigate my teenage years amid all the messy hair crises and burden of self-consciousness. My older brother is sixteen, as big as the doorframe, and trying to hide his excitement behind those moody bangs. My younger brother is just eight years old. He's the reason we still send our Christmas lists up the chimney, put out carrots for Rudolph, and hang out stockings in hope. Of course, he knows and probably does it for me really. I appreciate that.

My mother is in the kitchen, hands in fat oven gloves holding a tray of roast potatoes. Crispy on the outside, fluffy as dreams in the middle. Cheeks pink from the heat, or the pride, she's glad her brood isn't bickering today. On the one day of the year we're allowed to eat anything we want, all we want is Christmas dinner. Dad carves. I stand at the stone dividing wall between the kitchen and the dining space, ready to deliver the steaming promise to the table, which is laid carefully with a green cloth and candles.

I pause for a moment and take in the scene. My beloved grandma, snuffling under her party hat as the sherry takes effect. She won't be in that chair for many more dinners, and I wonder what she is thinking. My brothers act cool, but they are not too cool for Christmas. Soon we'll have our heads in exams, then be off to university and into our own lives, with boyfriends and girlfriends and spouses and children of our own. I watch Mum and Dad laughing about something, blurred at the edges by the cloud of steam from the turkey, and think that they won't always be this young. I wonder if they feel the shifting shape of the family, too.

I can't wait to grow up, yet I already want the rushing years to slow down. The unknowns and invitations of adult life are calling, but they can wait . . . for now. Because I want to be here, with these people, in this house, with this food. Today, at least. Together.

GATHERING WITH LOVED ONES

A calm Christmas does not have to be a small Christmas or even a quiet Christmas. Rather, it is one where you remove your known stressors, let go of perfection, and focus on what really matters to you. You might need to shave away a few traditions here, tweak some plans there, and spread out your social events. But doing so will help you achieve a better balance without missing out on the parts of Christmas you love most.

Much of the stress at this time of year comes from being pulled in many different directions and taking on the pressure of hosting at the end of a long year. One route to a calmer Christmas is to begin with some real honesty about who you want to spend time with. Then you can consider what type of gathering will allow you to connect properly, catch up, and show them how much you care. You might want to make space for moments alone with certain individuals, outside of group events. If you don't have the energy to host a large gathering, you could ask others to share the load, or attend someone else's event.

THE HALL OF CELEBRATION

Imagine that everyone you care about is gathered in a hall, decked out for the season. Now picture two large, overlapping circles on the floor, like a giant Venn diagram. Escort all the people you really want to see in person over Christmas into the circle on the left. Next, think about everyone with whom you want to exchange gifts, and picture them gathering in the circle on the right.

If there is anyone you want to both spend time with and exchange gifts with, envisage them moving to the center, where the two circles overlap.

If there is anyone left cheerfully milling around the edges of the two circles, glass of mulled wine in hand, perhaps, those are the people you can simply acknowledge or remember this year, perhaps with a Christmas card, a phone call, or even just a toast.

Of course, you care about all of these people and want to let them know it in some way. But the more people you place inside the circles, the more stressful your Christmas is likely to be, as you try to accommodate everyone.

Depending on your family dynamics, budget, and energy levels, you may be able to reduce Christmas stress by:

- Shifting some people from inside the circles to outside, knowing that simply acknowledging them (with a card, call, or toast) is enough.
- Minimizing the number of people in the central overlapping section (with whom you will both gather *and* exchange gifts). In your mind's eye, picture them stepping into the main part of one of the two circles (meaning you will choose to *either* gather *or* exchange gifts). You could agree to not exchange presents when you meet, or send them an early gift in lieu of hosting this year.
- Reducing the financial pressure associated with

accommodating those who are left in the center. For example, you could agree on an inexpensive gift theme, such as books, or decide to keep the menu simple.

All Christmas gatherings are not created equal. There are myriad ways to get together, with groups of various sizes in different places and spaces. It doesn't have to be all about partying, although it can be. With a little planning, you can even turn essential preparations into gatherings, and share the load in the process. And remember to leave some room for spontaneity. Some of the best gatherings are impromptu, last-minute affairs, but you need to be sufficiently relaxed and flexible to enjoy them.

CALM CONTEMPLATION: MINDFUL GATHERING

- Who do you *really* want to spend time with this year?
- Who might need your help and support this

year? For whom would your presence be a gift in itself?

- What, if anything, would you like to change about the role you tend to play when you gather with others?

SACRED TIME

Try to spend at least a few hours with each of the individuals who mean the most to you over the holidays. One of my favorite Christmas excursions was just me and my mum (and a bunch of strangers) singing carols in a candlelit cave in the Derbyshire village of Hope. We traveled by train, got lost, found our way with the help of some friendly locals, and ended up deep inside a mountain singing "Silent Night."

Use this sacred time to do something simple but special that will enable you to reconnect with each other. Go ice-skating, see the Christmas lights being switched on in your town, dig out your old turntable and play some records, volunteer at a soup kitchen, make something, or just have a long, intimate conversation.

If you can manage to carve out this special time with each of those you love, you are less likely to feel as if your whole Christmas has been hijacked, regardless of any obligations to host or attend events.

CHRISTMAS CAKE AND CINNAMON DREAMS

I'm six years old and careful with the big knife as I try to spread a layer of raspberry jam onto the heavy fruit cake. "That's right," Mum says kindly, even though I'm having little success. I then layer on the thick yellow marzipan, loving the feel of it—a bit like Play-Doh—as I push it over the rim of the cake. I break off a bit and snaffle it while Mum is reaching into the drawer for her rolling pin. If she sees, she doesn't say.

We drape a raft of royal icing over the top, then wrap around a long golden ribbon, and finish it off with a sprig of holly.

Food is the axis around which Christmas spins for most of us. Everyone has their festive favorites: bacon stolen off the top of the turkey; the annual batch

138

of homemade limoncello; clove-studded ham with spiced red cabbage; poached eggs on biscuits; cookies; smoked salmon; rabbit with potato dumplings; eggnog; mulled cider and wine; Grandma's cranberry sauce; the mother-in-law's mac and cheese; mushroom Wellington; and many more.

Holiday food is a source of pride and an expression of love, while Christmas dinner is probably the most anticipated meal of the year.

HOW A CHICKEN PIE
SAVED OUR CHRISTMAS

Centuries ago, long before refrigerators and mass-produced food, winter was a lean and challenging time. Nevertheless, feasting has always been an integral part of the holidays, with luxury versions of staples served up alongside special cuts of meat and other centerpieces, all lovingly prepared. *The Irish Countrywomen's Association Book of Christmas* is full of tales of puddings and cakes made well in advance and then sent, wrapped in greaseproof paper, on trains and boats all over the world.[1] One member even tells of a whole turkey sent from Tipperary to London, wrapped in pages from the *Wicklow People* newspaper. Food was—and still is—a central part of Christmas for many of us. If cooking up a huge traditional dinner for your entire family is your favorite part of Christmas, that is a wonderful thing. But for many, Christmas dinner is a source of stress.

As with so many aspects of modern life, expectations (and shopping lists) relating to festive fare have increased exponentially in recent years. The average UK household now spends £225 ($290) on food for December 25 alone.[2] No wonder there is so much pressure to "get it right." But do we really have to do it exactly the same way every year?

Half-Lebanese, half-Welsh mum-of-two Caroline McLannahan remembers her parents getting so worked up about Christmas Day cooking that she is now consciously casual about the whole event each year.

Growing up, I couldn't imagine a Christmas dinner without turkey, because that's what we always had. But all that changed in the course of a single conversation when our younger daughter was a newborn and our elder one was a toddler. We had recently moved into a new house and had several relatives over for Christmas dinner. Instead of requesting help, we took it all on ourselves. Mr. K spent most of the day in the kitchen, while I nursed the baby and tried to entertain everyone. As the last of our guests left, Mr. K and I realized we had hardly seen each other all day, aside from brief discussions about logistics. As we flopped onto the sofa and stared at the moon through the conservatory window, plates of leftovers in hand, we vowed that we would never do Christmas the same way again.

"By the way, I don't even like turkey," said Mr. K.

"Neither do I!" I exclaimed.

We discussed every detail of the day and realized two essential truths. First, we should have roped in our guests to help. Second, we should have arranged the day differently so we got outside for some fresh air—our favorite thing to do had been lost in all the chaos. In the weeks that followed, we had a few tricky but refreshing conversations with our guests, who all agreed it had not been ideal. Then we outlined a host of changes for the following year, perhaps most importantly regarding the main meal.

We made a radical decision to ditch the traditional

lunch and go with a simpler menu. So began a new tradition of cooking the filling for a pot pie on Christmas Eve, which meant we had plenty of time to go for a long walk on Christmas morning. When we returned home, we popped the pie in the oven and it was ready to serve in under an hour.

Perhaps we will reinstate the traditional roast when the girls are older, but for now our Christmas chicken pie feels just right . . . and it removes a massive amount of pressure.

> *Time-honored traditions are only worth maintaining if they honor your time and bring you pleasure.*

ANTICIPATION IS
THE SECRET INGREDIENT

Looking back at polar expeditions in the nineteenth and early twentieth centuries, it is clear that the prospect of Christmas dinner boosted morale and provided invaluable physical, emotional, and psychological nourishment. "Hair would be cut, beards shaved, and bodies, decks, and camps scrubbed and decorated in preparation for a ritualised time of relaxation," while the explorers looked forward to their double rations with "childish delight."[3]

During Robert Falcon Scott's expedition to Antarctica in 1901, seal liver, hot cocoa, pemmican (a mixture of concentrated fat and protein), biscuits, and spoonfuls of jam were all on the Christmas menu. Scott noted in his diary, "I had observed Shackleton ferreting about in his bundle out of which he presently produced a spare sock, and stowed away in the toe of that sock was a small round object about the size of a cricket ball, which when brought to light, proved to be a noble 'plum-pudding.'"[4] Imagine the elation of those explorers, each of whom probably had little more than a spoonful of pudding, but undoubtedly savored every morsel.

Planning Christmas meals well in advance not only reduces the likelihood of last-minute panic shopping but enhances the eating experience when the time finally comes. From an hour at the kitchen table surrounded by cookbooks to festive chitchat with the farm-shop owner, from floury faces and spoon-licking fun with little ones to the satisfaction of a freezer bursting with nourishing meals, there is much to enjoy in the process.

Last Christmas, we were living in a rented house while closing on our new home. We had expected to be in by November, so all our decorations were in storage. Consequently, our Christmas was even simpler than usual: just one room decorated with evergreens, fairy lights, and a few nature-inspired embellishments. Fortunately, that left plenty of time to focus on food.

I made gifts of stollen; jars of traditional English quince chutney, piccalilli, and lemon curd; and boxes of homemade chocolates. I baked Christmas cookies and gingerbread biscuits with clementine icing for the school cake sale. Then there was our family fare: the not-turkey pie, a chestnut loaf and fig jam, winter salads, candied peel dipped in chocolate, homemade granola, gallons of chicken stock for soups and risottos, jars of roasted nuts and seeds, tomato sauce, curries and a chili, and a wheelbarrow-load of roasted vegetables.

I was in my element chopping and pickling, baking and preserving. Leftovers stretched the nourishment much further. It never felt stressful, because the preparation was evenly distributed between late November and Christmas Eve, with baking days often accompanied by Christmas songs and a glass or two of mulled wine.

I loved adding handmade labels to jars, and had a deep sense of satisfaction from knowing that there were so many hearty suppers in the freezer. There was also plenty on hand for friends and neighbors who popped by. It was all so different from that chaotic Christmas just a few years before, and I learned that a little planning really does go a long way.

DECK THE HALLS

Among the black and bare trees we shook the snow from the undergrowth with frost-reddened fingers, seeking the sharp-spiked holly, bunches of laurel and ivy, cold clusters of moon-pale mistletoe. With these, our sisters transformed the familiar kitchen into a grotto of shining leaves, an enchanted bower woven from twigs and branches sprinkled with scarlet berries.

—Laurie Lee, *Village Christmas and Other Notes on the English Year*[5]

Twelve Tips for Stress-free Festive Food Preparation

1. Map out every event for which you plan to cook, either alone or with other people. Decide on a menu for each, remembering to include breakfast, lunch, and snacks if guests will be staying for several days. Ask your guests about any special dietary requirements and preferences well in advance. If thinking about it makes you feel anxious, find ways to simplify your plans or rope in some support.

2. Think about the cooking utensils and serveware you will need to cater for your guests. If you don't have enough of everything, and can't borrow it, the Black Friday sales at the end of November are a good opportunity to buy anything you need at a bargain price.

3. If you find cooking everything a bit too stressful, ask yourself the following questions:

- Which specific item or meal do you most associate with Christmas? Can you make it yourself with love, or buy the very best version of it? If this seems feasible, consider letting go of peripheral fare. This will save you time, energy, and money.

- Will your guests help? If you ask them to bring something, specify what you need, so you know what to expect and they don't have to guess.

- Can you make anything ahead of time and freeze or store it? Schedule time in your diary to do this. Perhaps set aside a whole Sunday for cooking main meals and/or a couple of evenings for baking and preserving.

- Could some of your homemade products make good gifts?

4. Write a complete list of the ingredients you need, check your cupboards to see what you already have, *then* do your shopping. When compiling your list, remember to include ingredients for healthy breakfasts, such as frozen fruit for smoothies, to give everyone a good start to the day.

$\longrightarrow$

5. To avoid the supermarket crowds, either order online or shop locally. Buying direct from growers, bakers, or independent shopkeepers makes it so much more special when it comes time for the meal.

6. If you buy too much, consider donating some of it to the local food bank.

7. If money is scarce, encourage your guests to contribute something, such as wine or dessert. If you have a large family, consider organizing a Christmas dinner fund, to be used by whoever is hosting. Plant-based dishes tend to be cheaper than meat or fish, so even if you do a small roast, be extra-generous with sides to fill plates. It will still feel like a special feast if you take extra care with the table settings and lighting, and radiate festive spirit.

8. Make a simple week-by-week plan for December, and a day-by-day plan for the week before Christmas. Include ideas for table decorations if these will need to be made in advance. If your schedule seems overwhelming, reduce the number of guests at your main gathering, make it more casual, invite people to stay for fewer days (or not at all), simplify your menu, or plan to eat out on occasion.

9. Batch cook and freeze casual, nutritious meals, such as warming stews, for eating between Christmas and New Year.

10. When cooking, put on your favorite apron and some festive music, rope in some help if possible, and try to enjoy it. Make a simple timeline counting backwards from when you want to serve, and set alarms on your phone for when each component needs to come out of the oven. If you plan it correctly, this can be a mindful experience as you melt into the smells, sights, textures, sounds, and, of course, tastes of your bubbling dishes.

11. Consider setting up festive party stations, so your guests can help themselves to drinks and snacks before the main event. Serve the meal itself in large bowls or on platters, or dishes straight from the oven, buffet style.

12. Finally, try to relax. Remember, your guests are all grateful for the effort you're making and they want to spend time with you.

There were only two occasions when my dad would stand on a ladder: to get the Christmas decorations down from a high shelf above the stairwell, and to put them back a few weeks later. One by one, the battered cardboard boxes would be passed down to my mum, standing at the bottom of the ladder, and then to a chain of us children until the baubles were finally delivered to their rightful place at the foot of the tree.

The most exotic Christmas decoration we ever had was a silver-and-blue expandable foil star. Lying flat, it was no more than a series of squares on top of one another, but when you picked up the hook at the center of the top layer, it stretched into a captivating lantern that caught the light as it twirled. That decoration was my dad's pride and joy. He had picked it up on a trip to Spain at what he thought was a bargain price . . . until he realized he had put the decimal point in the wrong place when doing the exchange-rate calculation. That made it the most expensive decoration we had ever seen. The most expensive in all of Europe, probably. We treated it with due reverence, as if it had the power to guide us all the way to Bethlehem, and it enjoyed pride of place above the dining table every Christmas from when I was eight until my parents moved some three decades later.

Decorating the home can become a lovely annual ritual. Whether done alone or with others, it can represent a special moment in the year—the point when Christmas truly begins. In fact, scientists have found that hanging Christmas decorations generates positive emotions and powerful memories of childhood.[6]

For centuries, people have brought light and life to the darkest days of winter by decorating their homes with candles, lamps, and evergreens. Holly and ivy are said to provide a sanctuary for fairies over the cold winter months. Meanwhile, that universal invitation to kiss—mistletoe—was traditionally harvested with a golden sickle, carried high and hung over doors to bring good luck.[7] Herbs have long been used symbolically in festive displays, including rosemary for remembrance and bay for valor.[8]

One of the true delights of our somewhat wild cottage garden is that it has everything we need to make a Christmas wreath: holly and ivy with an abundance of berries, hazel, bay, yew, willow, plenty of moss. Sometimes we even find pheasant feathers lying around.

If evergreens are in short supply where you live, you can usually forage them from local woods (requesting permission where necessary), or pay a visit to a local market, farm shop, or florist. There's no need to wait until late December to make a wreath. I usually adorn our front door with autumn delights from November onwards, and refresh our Christmas wreath for some seasonal cheer through January. This particular creative endeavor encourages you to get outside, use your hands, and take time out to make something really special.

Evergreens and berries are subtle signs of life when much of the garden is dying back. They represent hope, regeneration, and the spirit of life itself. Similarly, natural decorations are not showy or loud. Instead, they offer a warm welcome and a hint of potent midwinter magic.

LIGHTING THE WAY

Good lighting makes everything more magical, and fairy lights and candles (real or artificial) don't cost much. You don't need to invest in fancy new candlesticks—

wine bottles, old lanterns, even a block of wood with a few holes cut in it for tealights can work wonderfully. And fairy lights look good on everything—a tree, a branch, a gate, wrapped around the trinkets on your mantelpiece, in a mason jar as a portable lantern. Then there is firelight, of course, which offers warmth, too. Turn off your overhead lights, use these gentler methods instead, and see your rooms transformed.

And don't forget the outside of your home. Lamps by the front door send out a generous welcome, while solar-powered lights alongside paths and in trees are a gift to passersby.

LETTING GO OF PERFECT

See yourself as a custodian of Christmas. Notice the first scent of pine in the crisp December air as you wrap your hands gleefully around a mug of hot chocolate. Recognize how much goes into planning the gatherings, chivvying the relatives, thinking long and hard about gifts, saving the ribbon, stashing away the paper, writing the cards, stirring the soup, stacking the kindling, fluffing the cushions, knitting the stockings, and opening your home and heart to welcome the magic of the season.

In our efforts to create the "perfect" Christmas year in, year out, many of us overspend, overprepare, and overdo just about everything and end up so frazzled, stressed, and exhausted we cannot enjoy the wonder we have created. This year, let's do it differently. If you could do only *one* thing for each gathering, what would it be? Focus on that, do it brilliantly, and be relaxed about the rest.

Letting go of the notion of the perfect Christmas is not about lowering your expectations, but changing them. Try exchanging the word "perfect" for something else—a *memorable* Christmas, a *lovely* Christmas, or a *special* Christmas, perhaps.

Remember that each and every Christmas is as unique as a snowflake, and that Christmas is likely to be much calmer if you can be flexible with your plans, ideas, and responses. Create the circumstances you need for a great Christmas, but then try to go with the flow and make the best of whatever unfolds.

PREPARING YOURSELF

Christmas happens all around us, whether we choose to participate or not. But when we organize a gathering, we invite it into our homes, along with our guests. As soon as those guests step inside, they will experience both the physical environment (the temperature, the lighting, the decorations, etc.) and the emotional environment (the ambience you have created). As the host, you can make that environment more welcoming, and you can encourage connection among the guests, but you cannot dictate their behavior or mood. Accepting that is the key to a calmer frame of mind.

Before your guests arrive—or before the rest of the family wakes up on Christmas Day—switch your focus from what you haven't yet done, to all that you *have* done to prepare for this. Think about all you have created in the kitchen and on the wrapping table, and all the care that has gone into decorating and otherwise preparing for this moment, and hold those offerings close as you open the front door or step into the day. Know that there will be so much gratitude for what you have done, even if people don't find the words to tell you. So, take a deep breath before it all begins, and choose to relax.

CALM IN THE CHAOS

The word "calm" derives from the late-Latin *cauma* ("heat"), and stems from the practice of resting during the heat of the day. If you are feeling stressed by the heat of Christmas, try the following exercise.

CALM CONTEMPLATION: CALMING YOUR TRIGGERS

We are often acutely aware of what is stressing us out, but that knowledge is rarely sufficient to lessen the impact. However, a simple exercise might help.

Sketch out the table below. Add your personal stressors to the left-hand column, such as rude people in busy shopping malls or passive-aggressive comments

156

from one of your guests. Then list your typical responses in the right-hand column. Try to be very specific (and honest): for example, "sarcasm" or "snappiness."

	Things that trigger stress	My usual response
1		
2		
3		
4		
5		

Now, sketch out a second table and write *exactly the same entries* in the left-hand column as you did in the first table. This time, though, in the right-hand column, choose an alternative response that will help you relax. Here are some suggestions:

- Take a deep breath
- Place a hand on my heart
- Close my eyes for a moment
- Silently say "Thank you" for this reminder to remain calm

	Things that I will now use to trigger calm	My new response
1		
2		
3		
4		
5		

Next time you come into contact with one of your stress triggers, remind yourself that it can be a calm trigger and choose the second type of response.

MINDFUL HOSTING

Visualizing your gathering before it happens can make a huge difference. Many of us hope everything will run smoothly but presume there will be chaos, and this can become a self-fulfilling prophecy. So, instead, try to visualize a calm, relaxed event. Here are tips for being a mindful host, to pave the way for a mellow experience for you and an enjoyable event for your guests.

How to Be a Mindful Host

- Consider what single aspect of Christmas your guests might most like to experience. They will be delighted if you include the one element that really matters to them.

- Ask for any special dietary requirements or preferences well in advance, as well as any unusual daily routines.

- Share the load of preparing and cooking. Be specific about what you need your guests to bring or do. Invite them to bring reusable containers so they can take home leftovers.

- If one of your guests has had a really hard time this year but might not want to talk about it in front of a large group, you could leave a welcome card on their pillow. On the card, perhaps explain that you are always available for a chat, and that they shouldn't feel obliged to join in with any activities if they are uncomfortable.

- If you want to steer the conversation in a par-

→

ticular direction or avoid a potentially divisive subject, consider making your intentions known when you send out the invitations. For example, you could invite your guests to "A Christmas dinner to honor . . . and share stories from the past year" or "Festive fun and feasting (politics-free zone!)."

- If you want to limit screen time, tell people of your policy well in advance.
- Take some time to prepare your guests' rooms. Think about the little luxuries of a good B&B: a spare blanket, magazines, a jug of water, fresh towels. Perhaps leave a Christmas decoration on their bed along with an invitation to come and hang it on your tree once they have unpacked to mark the start of the celebrations. Making your guests feel truly welcome, preparing a restful space for them to sleep, and letting them know they are not obliged to spend every minute with the whole group will put them at ease.
- Create a small, quiet corner to which you (and your guests) can retreat, even if only for a few minutes.

- Take a few deep breaths just before your visitors are due to arrive.
- Keep your mood light, and don't drink too much.
- Plan some fun activities: a treasure hunt, board games, pin the nose on the reindeer, a long walk, or a festive singalong.
- Let people help and try not to fuss.
- If you feel anxious, imagine all your worries as a tangled set of fairy lights. Step back, look at them as separate from you, then imagine untangling them slowly.
- The hours will go in a flash. Savor it. Make time to talk to people, as well as serve them food and drink.
- If you start to feel stressed, make yourself a hot drink, close your eyes, and feel the shape of the mug as the warmth seeps through your skin and into your bones, up your arms, and around your heart. Then take a deep breath and open your eyes.
- Once your guests have left, take a moment to enjoy the lingering good energy.

DEALING WITH CONFLICT

Family gatherings tend to be a strange mix of inter-generational, complex dynamics, often fueled by too much alcohol, that play out in a confined space for an entire day or even longer.

As guests arrive with their gifts, they may also bring old wounds, assumptions, or bitterness. They may pass judgment on your way of life. They could well be nervous. Or they might want a day of peace, love, and laughter at the end of a hard year. Everyone has their issues, and they all coalesce in an emotional pot of Christmas stew.

On December 27 last year, I overheard two dog-walkers discussing their respective Christmases. "Honestly, on Christmas Day, I couldn't breathe," said the first. "I wish I had just stepped outside for a few minutes." Something so simple can make a huge difference in the midst of tension or conflict, but we often neglect to do it. Instead, we allow ourselves to get embroiled in heated conversations and arguments.

Below are some tips to help you deal with divisive situations.

SILENCE AND SNOWFALL

There's a place I like to go whenever I'm feeling stressed or overwhelmed—a forest in northern Japan, deep in the mountains. The snow is thick on the ground, dampening every sound, so all I hear is birdsong and my own breathing. Sometimes the wind blows and the snow drifts, but I am sheltered by the trees.

It's been ten years since I stood in that forest, but I often visit in my mind. It never fails to calm me.

Even if you are blessed with the most congenial family and love every aspect of Christmas, there is sure to come a time when you need to step away. Cultivating your own mental space of silence and snowfall—or whatever is most restful for you—can be a lifeline when the festivities get to be too much.

You could also create a calming physical space in your home—perhaps a quiet room, a secluded corner with a beanbag and a book, or a comfy chair and a bag of sewing. If guests are staying, invite them to use it. This can be especially helpful when children are visiting. Quiet music and some paper and pens for drawing

Minimizing Tension Over the Holidays

These tips can help reduce the likelihood of conflict over Christmas:

- Remember, you don't have to accept every invitation, especially if you suspect the atmosphere might turn acrimonious.
- If you do accept, be realistic about how long you should stay. For instance, it might be fine to join for lunch, but staying overnight would be too much. Or perhaps you should just pop in for an hour in the afternoon. You might want to team up with a close friend and plan an exit strategy if the conversation gets too heated or strays into unwelcome territory.
- If you are the host, and are nervous about potential conflict, be upfront about the duration of your invitation.
- It is your right and responsibility to set any

ground rules, such as no political debates in your home. You can do this in a serious or a lighthearted way.

- Where possible, build movement into the time you will be spending together, such as a long country walk. Getting people moving usually helps to lift the mood.

- If this particular group has been plagued by conflict in the past, try to work out why and how you might minimize the likelihood of it raising its head again. For example, if it tends to be initiated or exacerbated by alcohol, how about serving mocktails rather than cocktails, or doing something that does not involve drinking?

- If one individual often looks for an argument, think of conversation starters that will lead them away from challenging topics. Imagine you are meeting them for the first time. What would you ask them about their life or their memories of Christmas?

- If you expect some unwelcome questions, plan your answers and work out how to move on to

→

other topics. Preempting awkward conversations will give you more confidence and help you stay calm if a difficult topic does arise.

- If you are a guest, is there anything you can do to help the host remain calm?
- Afterwards, reflect on what happened and try to figure out how to handle it next time, or whether there should be a next time.

can help calm little ones (and grown-ups) at the end of an exciting day.

WHEN CHRISTMAS COMES

You have made it to Christmas! Whatever kind of a year you have had, you are still here. On Christmas Eve, after all the preparations have been made and before the big day is upon you, take a moment to breathe, reflect, and be thankful.

Anglo-Saxon pagans celebrated December 24 as *Modranicht*—"Night of the Mothers"—which resonates particularly strongly with me, as I was in labor on Christmas Eve a few years ago.

These days, I have my own Christmas Eve ritual. Prior to a quiet dinner with my husband, I cuddle my daughters, and reflect on that Christmas I became a mother. Then I light a candle and give thanks to my own mother and the women before her, to the gift of motherhood, and to everyone who is offering a mothering influence to others, in whatever capacity that may be.

It is a lovely moment to reflect on your relationships with matriarchal figures, and to honor the nurturing instincts that have helped you prepare for this festive season. It is also the perfect time to breathe in the calm that settles around twilight on Christmas Eve.

The Snow Globe

If you ever feel anxious or stressed in the middle of a crowd, or even in a small group of people, imagine you are in a snow globe. There is a sphere of protection all around you, and inside, snow is gently falling. You can see what is happening outside, but the noise is muffled, and you can rest in stillness as the Christmas whirlwind spins.

Practice mindfulness in the midst of the rush. Focus on the specific sensory details of your immediate environment—the feel of a cup in your hand, the temperature of the air—and allow the snow globe to insulate you from the sensory overload outside.

CHAPTER 6

Honoring the Melancholy

DEALING WITH SADNESS, LOSS, AND LONELINESS

Popular culture paints a picture of Christmas as a joyous time when families come together to feast and celebrate life in a convivial atmosphere. But that is far from reality for many of us.

Exploring loneliness, sadness, and grief at Christmas from the points of view of those who need support and those who are willing and able to provide it is not a case of "us" and "them." We have all been both helpers and helped at one time or another. Everything comes into sharp focus at this time of year, with life's milestone events—births, marriages, empty nesting, illnesses, recovery, deaths—gaining added poignancy, especially when something has shaken our lives since the previous Christmas.

Loneliness, sadness, and grief are universal human emotions that are neither straightforward nor predictable.

We tend to associate loneliness at Christmas with elderly people, yet a staggering number of millennials report feeling lonely at this time of year, and many people in midlife tell of loneliness experienced inside marriages, or as bonds of friendship have weakened over time.

Sadness comes in many forms, including a general melancholy that sweeps in with the season. If people we love are far away—studying abroad, serving in the military, having moved, or estranged, perhaps—their absence is often felt most strongly at this time of year.

Grief may be for loved ones we have lost, for gatherings we will never attend again, for children we never had, or for relationships that have turned sour.

Often the best we can do is honor the melancholy and be there when needed. Go easy on yourself . . . and on others.

DARK DAYS
AND LONELY NIGHTS

It's a dark, rainy night early in December, and my head is resting against the filthy window of a double-decker bus while I watch the raindrops falling down the glass at the end of a long day. I'm a postgraduate student in Bath, a city in England founded by the Romans as a thermal spa, riding the top deck back to my flat after class. The bus stops for a moment, and the raindrops take on an orange glow. They are reflecting the light from chandeliers blazing through the night from the second-floor drawing room of one of the elegant Georgian houses on the hill. I see the silhouettes of a woman in a dress and a man holding a glass of wine by one window, and a group of people chatting and laughing by another. It's a storybook scene, and I am the reader, unable to make my way into the page and participate. I can't tell whether the knot in my stomach is hunger or longing. Not for a Georgian drawing room and chandeliers, but simply for an invitation.

I felt so lonely that year. Utterly absorbed in my studies, I had made few friends. Everything about the countdown to Christmas in that beautiful city seemed to tap me on the shoulder and remind me of the fact that I was single and living on a tight budget. Colleagues were heading out to the Christmas market for mulled wine after work, people were out shopping, every restaurant was filled with patrons in party hats popping champagne corks. Meanwhile, I spent a lot of time in the bookshop.

As term was drawing to a close, in a translation study group with some of my Japanese classmates, one of them started to cry. That set off some of the others. With the release of tears came reluctant admissions of how much they were all missing their families. Only then did I realize that they too had been wandering through the streets of the same city, feeling a similar way to me, only their yearning for home was even deeper than my own, given the thousands of miles between them and their loved ones.

I invited them all to my parents' house the following weekend. We baked Christmas biscuits, ate a roast dinner, and laughed more than we had since meeting each other at the beginning of term. By looking up and out, I realized I was not alone, and that solidarity made all the difference. I was in need of connection, and in the process I discovered others who needed it, too.

There is a stoicism in our culture that has kept the lid on loneliness for far too long. Thankfully, though, people are finally starting to talk about it. According to the UK government, which has had a Minister for Loneliness since 2017, loneliness is as detrimental to your health as smoking fifteen cigarettes a day,[1] and more than three-quarters of us feel lonely at one time or another.[2] In the United States, rates of loneliness have more than doubled in the past forty years: it is estimated that some forty-three million US adults over the age of forty-five suffer from chronic loneliness.[3]

However, although it is pervasive in society, loneliness is not always visible. Of all the stories I gathered while researching this book, some of the most affecting came from people who felt lonely within their marriages, or in large groups. They would go through the motions at Christmas but feel empty inside, or suffer a sudden realization that they didn't really know—or like—those with whom they were spending time.

Some people felt lonely as they clung on to the ragged end of a friendship. Others shared that they had few friends to call on, often because single parenthood or a demanding job or years of travel had caused bonds to stretch and eventually break. For some, the chill wind of loneliness blows in through the front door whenever their children leave to spend part of Christmas with an ex-spouse. For others, it lingers all season long now that their life partner has departed or their relatives have moved far away.

> *When you're down, reach out.*
> *When you're up, reach out.*

Loneliness is an aspect of the human experience that we all dwell in from time to time, and it is exacerbated when we measure ourselves against other people and feel inadequate. Many of us are loath to reach out due to fear of rejection, which causes us to retreat further, feel even more lonely, and deny ourselves the medicine of human contact we really need.

HOW TO DEAL
WITH LONELINESS

If you are feeling lonely, try these tips, which I have curated from my own experience, and from the experiences of those in my community.

- Take extra care of yourself in terms of nutrition and exercise. Make food an event by planning your menus, then use the meals themselves as opportunities to practice mindfulness in their preparation and eating.
- Reach out and talk with others about how you're feeling. Remember, almost everyone feels lonely at some time in their life.
- Broaden your horizons by listening to podcasts, reading books, attending lectures, and exploring new music.
- Minimize your screen time and be mindful about how you are using social media.
- Meditate, do yoga, or attend a mindfulness workshop.

- Reflect on whether your sense of loneliness is telling you to pay more attention to certain aspects of your life.

- List the advantages of your current situation. If you find yourself complaining about something, add the words "so I can . . ." at the end of the sentence to flip it into an opportunity.

- Seek out an inspiring book, then settle down to read it as if there is nothing in the world you would rather be doing.

- Revisit the Five Stories of Christmas in Chapter 1 and consider how you might honor those that matter most to you. This will provide a focal point for the holiday season and give you a reason to reach out to someone else who values the same stories.

- If limited finances are preventing you from attending expensive events, be creative about the way you gather with others. Perhaps invite someone to join you for a walk or some Christmas crafting.

- Decorate the outside of your home with lights to raise the spirits of passersby. A lantern by the front door or fairy lights around the window can be your gift to strangers. This simple act can forge strong connections with neighbors and the rest of the local community as it sends a message of friendliness and approachability.[4]

- If you are missing people who live far away, arrange an online video chat. You could keep the connection open while you cook dinner or decorate the tree.

- If being in the house feels oppressive, get outside. Seek out nature wherever you are.

- Give yourself something to look forward to. Maybe treat yourself to some art supplies, register for a half marathon, or sign up for an evening class.

- Be kind to others, and to yourself.

We cannot know the precise nature of someone else's emotional experience at this time of year—the shadow of loss, the beating heart of sorrow, the searing pain of loneliness, the dull ache of wishing things were different—but we can be mindful of what it might feel like, based on our own experience, careful observation, and empathy.

HOW TO HELP OTHERS COPE

There are a number of ways in which you might help other people to cope with their loneliness at this time of year:

- Extend an invitation. If it is rejected, try sending a second one for a smaller or more casual event, possibly involving just the two of you. Alternatively, you could ask for assistance choosing ingredients at the market, or with the cooking, for example. But don't push: give space where it's needed.

- If they accept your invitation to a gathering, ask if there are any topics they would rather avoid, then stay alert during the event and change the subject if necessary.

- Once you have made arrangements, do your utmost not to cancel.

- Remember, loneliness is often invisible. Most people will not tell you that they are suffering, so you might have to pay close attention. If you

detect something is wrong, let them know you
are available to listen. Then, if they choose to
open up, do just that—listen—without offering unsolicited advice. Simply say that you
empathize.

- Check in regularly, remain patient, and let them
know you will still be there after the holidays.
- Smile at strangers, especially those who seem in
need of a pick-me-up.
- Take care with social media posts and think about
the message you want to convey before posting or
uploading anything.
- Let people know you appreciate them. Your words
could be just the boost they need.

AN EMPTY CHAIR

*Last year the husband of a friend of mine passed away in the
night, seemingly out of nowhere, at the age of forty. Jessica
is an artist, and at the time had a toddler, and was expecting
a second child. Shocked at the news, Jess's creative community responded immediately, raising $60,000 to support Jess*

and her children in the years ahead. Their generosity was almost overwhelming.

Yet, few people knew that her heart had already begun to break two months before her husband Ryan's death, when she discovered that he had a hidden and destructive drug addiction. By the time she found out, it was already too late.

The devastation of losing her husband does not reside alone in her fractured heart. A heavy guilt lurks there too, an unwelcome response to the sense of relief she feels at no longer having to live in fear of the addiction. She told me:

It's painful to think back on the months after Ryan's death. I loved Coen. I held Coen. I cried a lot. In the shower, in the car, on the front porch. I let myself feel whatever I needed to feel. I was numb at times. I had to let people help me.

Having to take care of Coen through it all was a huge gift. I had to get up and be a good mother every day.

I let the waves of painful emotion move through me and didn't try to stop them. Each time I did that I learned again and again that they wouldn't last forever.

I remember the moment I first realized we would be spending Christmas without Ryan. I was moving some things around on the mantel above the fireplace, and I noticed the tiny nails we used to hang out our stockings.

My mom visited us a couple of weeks before Christmas and we spent a day making cookies like we did when I was a kid. It was wonderful. We laughed so hard that day, and I remember thinking how good it felt.

It felt good to do the holiday things I love, even though it was so different. The trauma of Ryan's death and the events leading up to it were still fresh in my mind at Christmas, and I think it might take some time for me to see beyond those painful memories and remember the wonderful years we shared before that.

It's only when Jess tells me this that I finally have a true sense of what she's feeling. We can never really know what's going on in someone else's heart, because everyone's pain is different. It assumes its own unique form as it evolves over time.

> *We don't always want a merry Christmas,*
> *and that's fine.*

All too often, especially during the festive season, we make assumptions about someone who has suffered a recent loss, then try to improve their mood on the basis of those assumptions. It can be more helpful to simply ask how they would like to celebrate—if at all—and how their loss should be acknowledged. Similarly, if you have suffered a loss, ask yourself what you need this year. If your answer is radically different from how you usually celebrate, that's okay.

Grief can have a strange effect on the passage of time. A loss may leave you feeling stuck, unable to move forward, yet in other ways life keeps trundling along. Sometimes everyday distractions take over; other times the grief whips you back to the moment when life changed. And things get even more complicated as nostalgia builds over Christmas. You may feel simultaneously sad and joyous, present in the moment and lost in the past. Christmas can stir reflection and heighten our emotions. It can be both a challenging and precious time.

We will all experience an empty chair at the table some day. Eventually, that empty chair will be ours. Christmas can be an opportunity to pause and acknowledge our mortality, to give thanks, and to remember.

CHRISTMAS WITHOUT YOU

I hope the following story will bring some comfort, especially if you have suffered a loss this year. Please remember you are not alone, and you will make it through.

> I lost my husband to cancer on December 21, 2016.
> Phill and I had always loved Christmas. Our record
> was seven fully decorated trees. I'd nursed Phill at
> home and he died in my arms next to the twinkling
> lights we both loved so much. Christmas will always
> be special because it reminds me of him.
>
> —Gillian Moakes

All the tips for dealing with loneliness (see "How to Deal with Loneliness," p. 175) are equally valid for dealing with grief. In addition, practice saying "No, thanks" or "Not right now," depending on how you feel; or "Maybe," if you don't know how you will feel. Recognize that Christmas might be different this year. Meet up with others in a similar situation if you feel it will help. Find a way to honor or pay tribute to the person who is absent, and bring them into your observance of Christmas if you feel ready to do so. And ask for help in specific ways. People are often desperate to help, but don't know how.

Similarly, all the tips for supporting someone who is struggling with loneliness are equally valid for helping those who have lost a loved one, as are the guidelines for being a mindful host (see Chapter 5). In addition, try to understand and accept that Christmas will be different for them this year. Recognize what they are going through, and extend a little extra compassion. Invite them to join in, but give them space if they need it.

ANOTHER KIND OF GRIEF

The grief of involuntary childlessness—which is largely unacknowledged in our culture—also intensifies at this time of year. With so many reminders that Christmas is often a child-centered celebration, along with probing and insensitive questions at family get-togethers, the season can be a real challenge for anyone who wants children, but does not have any.

While sharing their stories for this book, many people mentioned the sadness and sense of loss they have felt through not being able to have children. They wrote with desperately heavy hearts of miscarriages, stillbirths, and failed IVF treatment. What I noticed most, though, was how quietly they spoke of their grief response. People who had lost relatives or friends were very open about their grief and how it made Christmas challenging, but for those grieving the loss of a hoped-for future with children, their tone was hushed, as if they did not want to take up too much space in the Christmas conversation.

Yet, grief is grief, whether it is for lost loved ones, lost hope, or lost futures that will never come to pass. One interpretation of the Portuguese word *saudade* seems to capture the latter emotion beautifully. The scholar Aubrey Bell defines it as "a vague and constant desire for something that does not and probably cannot exist, for something other than the present."[5]

This feeling can be especially acute at Christmas-time, in part due to the relentless pressure to remain cheerful, so be mindful and attentive to your loved ones' experiences.

MAKING SPACE FOR JOY

Christmas has a strange power to root us in the moment while also transporting us somewhere else. It brings to mind a haiku by Matsuo Bashō:

> Even in Kyoto—
> hearing the cuckoo's cry—
> I long for Kyoto.[6]

We can feel nostalgic about Christmas even when we are right in the middle of it. If our current experience does not match up to our memories of Christmases past, or what we think we should be experiencing because of what we see on social media or in the movies, we can lose ourselves in the gap. This leads to disconnection from the here and now, and sadness. However, if we can find a way to inhabit the season, perhaps by identifying with a particular person, place, or moment, we can rebuild the bonds of connection and feel part of Christmas once more.

A friend told me that her father was the heart and soul of Christmas in their household. He would write poetry and perform sketches as a gift to everyone on Christmas Day. Now that he has passed away, my friend has decided to take the baton and continue the tradition in his honor. I love this idea.

Two billion people celebrate Christmas each year. Imagine if each of us were to reach out to just one other person—be it a friend, a relative, or a stranger—over the holidays. If we were to share what is real and true to us, and what we need most, the effect on our collective emotional health would be profound.

A DIFFERENT KIND
OF CHRISTMAS DAY

Sometimes, the best gift we can give ourselves is permission to experience a completely different kind of Christmas. Many people shared how a break in tradition has been refreshing or healing for them. Here are just a few examples:

> Last year, I ran away from it all to India and spent it with seventeen yoga people on my teacher training course. There was no pressure. I felt a sense of compassion, kindness, and love.
>
> —Sharon

> I like to volunteer. I don't have much in life past the basics but, having worked in a refugee camp, I know it is enough, and I like to give back.
>
> —Paul

> When my son was three, my mother lost her battle with cancer. The physical loss was huge. A couple of

years later, my son's father and I split up and my son was going to be spending Christmas with him and his family. Rather than dreading being on my own, I knew I needed to wake up on Christmas morning and just be free to cry instead of making everything wonderful for my son. That Christmas, I grieved for all the Christmases I would no longer spend with my mother.

—Mary-Anne

If you know you will be facing a different kind of Christmas this year, whether through choice or not, think about how you want to spend it. How will you make it special? For example, is it an opportunity for reflection and self-care, creativity, or working on a personal project?

*Give yourself permission
to do something different.*

CALM CONTEMPLATION: PREPARING YOURSELF EMOTIONALLY FOR CHRISTMAS

- How will you prepare yourself for any feelings of sadness over the holidays?
- How might you reach out to others for emotional support? Who might be able to support you and what could they do?
- How might you offer emotional support to others? Who might need it and what could you do?

A CHRISTMAS WISH

However you choose to spend Christmas this year, I wish this for you:

May you know you are loved.

May you let others know you love them.

May you be safe, and offer shelter.

May you be open to your sadness, and welcome joy.

May you receive whatever you need.

PART 3

Manifestation: After Christmas

CHAPTER 7

Savoring the "Hush"

These are the days in between. The liminal space that hovers beyond the festivities and before the fresh New Year. A time of long walks, hot coffees, languid lounging with leftover chocolates, adding birthday dates to the new diary, telephone catch-ups, old memories, new plans, making time, telling stories, everything on pause.

WRAPPING YOURSELF IN THE CLOAK OF LATE DECEMBER

Have you noticed that something very special happens between Christmas and New Year? For a few days, a portal to another world opens up. Everything is quieter, less rushed, gentler in this secret place. Peering through the doorway, I always imagine there will be snow, although the sky usually offers knitted fog and dull winter sunshine. Nevertheless, calm descends as we catch a glimpse of a slower life away from all the deadlines and to-do lists. I call this time the "Hush," and I encourage you to savor it.

The hard work of Christmas is over for another year. There are no more cards to write or presents to wrap. New Year's Eve is a few days away, and many people are still off work.

If you have the luxury of some time off, you can eat leftover Christmas pudding for breakfast. You can leave emails unanswered in your inbox and spend hours playing board games. You can go for a long walk through muddy fields, then sit in a country pub all evening telling stories. You can go to bed early, or stay up late and sleep in till noon. You can answer the door at three in the afternoon in your pajamas. You can spend all day in the kitchen, cooking up vats of leek-and-potato soup and hearty casseroles, allowing your mind to wander as you stir slowly. You can take a stroll by the sea and eat an ice cream on an empty beach. You can clean your house from top to bottom or ignore the mess. You can putter in your garden, meditating on the winter silhouettes. Or you can dream and scheme, plot and plan for the year ahead.

The Hush is a precious time. We face so much change in the course of an average year, in the wider world and in our own lives. We endure a barrage of headlines, political turmoil, social injustice, dead-lines, hirings and firings, career shifts, health scares, births, marriages, deaths and breakups, house moves, and fluctuating friendship dynamics. It's one thing after another, all coming at us with barely a moment to pro-cess any of it. Then we fling ourselves into festivities. It's no wonder everything tends to catch up with us over the holidays, so it's crucial to give ourselves the time and space to wind down, switch off, and relax.

Starting on December 26, there is a fleeting pause when time bends and magic hovers between the book-ends of the season. The Norwegians call it *romjul*, from the old Norse, meaning "half-holy."[1] My friend Ingrid told me how much of Norway grinds to a halt between Christmas and New Year. She explained, "The shops are closed. There are days when you can't buy booze. It's all about friends and family. On our island, we go from house to house sharing buffets." It's not only half-holy but half-paced. "We must . . ." and "We should . . ." are abandoned in favor of "Shall we . . . ?" and "We could . . ." Spontaneity and softness become the order of the day.

If we keep the activity and volume levels high all the way to New Year, hosting a houseful of guests without a break, hunting out bargains in packed shopping malls or rushing back to work too soon, we miss a vital but rare opportunity to reflect and learn, honor and grieve, rest and recuperate.

Before marriage and children, I would often spend these days in an almost empty office, getting plenty done but feeling robbed of precious time. Now I take a complete break between Christmas and New Year, and encourage everyone on my team to do the same. No meetings or online classes are scheduled, and there is very little social media posting. It's good for everyone.

January will be here before we know it, after all. So, instead of rushing towards it, let's meander for a few days, giving our minds and hearts a chance to assimilate and process all that's happened over the past twelve months. This is a wonderful time to nurture your own energy, marvel at nature, and recharge.

There are practical things you can do—and avoid—to make the most of these magical few days.

CARVE OUT TIME FOR YOURSELF

The Hush is one of my favorite times of the year. I set aside a day for myself, away from commercial noise and work pressure, so my brain can rest and my imagination run free. It's both an escape from the real world and a glimpse of what that world can be.

There's no right or wrong way to go about this, but you might want to try one of the following suggestions to enjoy some time for yourself.

A DAY IN NATURE

Although catching up on sleep can be beneficial, too much can have a jetlag effect when the time comes to resume your normal routine. So pause and rest by all means, but try to maintain a regular sleep pattern and get some exercise. A restorative, refreshing day in

197

nature can work wonders in terms of brushing away the cobwebs and brightening your spirit.

There is a particular stillness in nature at the end of December—a stripped-back beauty that may seem bleak but actually conceals the first stirrings of new life. It can be deeply comforting to contemplate the circle of life and gain an understanding of the value of this pause for nurturing fresh growth in the spring.

According to Callum Saunders, features editor of *Creative Countryside* magazine:

> The countryside is a wily and wonderful teacher, if only we make the time to stop and listen to its rhythms. To linger is to submit fully to the moment, free of distraction: an immersion that draws you beneath the surface of the obvious and breathes new life into your understanding of place, space and time.[2]

A DIGITAL DETOX DAY

Switching off your phone for twenty-four hours (or longer) can transform your state of mind.[3] Try taking a break from emails, social media, and even phone calls, podcasts, and music, and notice the difference when you spend time being really present, paying attention to real-life conversations, and using all your senses as you move through the day.

If you find it difficult to keep your phone switched off, give yourself something to do. Go for a run. Do yoga. Bake bread. Read cookbooks. Take a bath. Drink a pot of warming tea. Sketch instead of taking photos. Write in your journal instead of keying notes into your tablet. When you feel a pull to check a device, observe the feeling, then let it go. Don't succumb to it. After a while, the urge will fade and you will feel more closely connected to all that is going on around you, with a renewed sense of control over the pace of your day.

Combining this with time in nature will amplify your sense of well-being.

A DREAMING DAY

Visit a favorite café, journal in hand, for a day of dreaming. Watch the steam as it rises from your latte while rain drums on the window and you settle into the cozy room. Think of it as a safe place to be with your thoughts about all that is and all that might be.

Dream alone or with whoever shares your life. Let your mind run free on the page or have long, juicy conversations about what you love about your life right now . . . and what you'd like to change.

A CREATIVE DAY

I love to write during this time of year. In fact, I tend to start writing my books between Christmas and New Year. Set aside a day for something creative: painting, crafting, poetry, journaling, making music, calligraphy, cooking. Or you could sketch out a new garden design, draft a book proposal, or create a vision board.

Try anything that allows you to use your creativity, and access the quiet place that lies beyond your noisy mind.

A SORT-OUT-MY-LIFE DAY

Since my early twenties, I have taken a full day near the end of each year to get on top of all the admin that gets in the way of everything else. I call it a sort-out-my-life day. It usually involves reams of paper spread all over the floor, endless cups of tea, a fair few sighs, some boring paperwork, and, ultimately, a tremendous sense of accomplishment.

Clearing the decks of all those annoying little jobs that you usually put off allows you to focus on more important—or enjoyable—matters as you enter the New Year.

A helpful by-product of this process is that you will often find ways to save money—or claim some back—which is always a blessing after Christmas.

The Hush is a great time to:

- pay any outstanding bills
- check all automatic payments and standing orders to ensure you aren't paying for a service you no longer receive
- return unwanted gifts
- draft a budget for the following year
- organize files and papers, ensure important documents are up-to-date, and check you are getting the best deals on your phone, energy, home insurance, etc.
- back up photos, videos, and other files
- write thank-you notes and a gratitude list

A SORT-OUT-MY-HOUSE DAY

Which camp are you in: the "every decoration must come down the day after Christmas" camp, or the "everything stays up until Twelfth Night (or longer)" camp? I veer between the two from year to year, depending on how early the decorations went up and how much I feel like I need a fresh start.

Either way, a sort-out-my-house day can be a wonderful way to declutter both your space and your mind. Here are some suggestions:

- Take down your decorations and pack them away carefully, storing delicate ornaments in old egg boxes and wrapping fairy lights around an old card to prevent them from getting tangled.
- Consider packing away the most Christmassy decorations (such as bright red ornaments) while retaining those that celebrate midwinter (such as evergreens). Leave some lights to twinkle in the house and garden to preserve the magic for a little longer.
- If you have piles of Christmas presents lying around, transfer them to the correct rooms—children's toys in their bedrooms, toiletries in the bathroom, etc.—to clear your living space.
- If you received unwanted gifts that you can't return, start a present box (for regifting throughout the year) or pay a visit to Goodwill.
- Paint a wall. Tend to house plants. Frame some photos.
- Flip your mattresses. Check your smoke alarms.

Clean your fridge. Do other small maintenance jobs around the house.

- Do winter jobs in the garden, like pruning trees, checking on greenhouse heaters, and harvesting seasonal vegetables.
- Give everywhere a good clean. If you travel during this time, it will feel great to return to a tidy, fresh home.

HOT CHOCOLATE AND HIBERNATION

It's December 28 and I'm sitting in a low leather armchair at the local café. I am here to write and don't mean to eavesdrop, but the coffee shop is tiny and the greetings warm and loud.

A ham sandwich on soft brown bread is my excuse for hanging around. French mustard and winter lettuce leaves from a local farm make the sandwich special, and I enjoy it with a pot of steaming tea. Later, perhaps I'll treat myself to a mug of coffee, so I can linger a while longer.

There are seasonal hugs between the owners and the customers, ear rubs for damp dogs, handmade treats in

*brown paper bags tied with a Christmas ribbon and dis-
creetly handed to the most loyal clients.*

*I overhear old friends sharing details of what they ate on
Christmas Day—ham with figs, homemade stollen, roast
parsnips to die for, and the best sloe gin you've ever tasted,
apparently. Then a torrent of generous questions:*

*"I was thinking of you cooking turkey for fifteen. How
did it go?"*

*"Did Elsie appreciate that wonderful photo album you
made her?"*

"Dinner tomorrow at our place?"

*Closing time comes, but no one wants to head into the
cold, so there's a coffee shop lock-in. The laughter builds
behind the steamed-up windows. The world is on hold.*

This can be a wonderful time to connect with family and friends in a relaxed atmosphere, far away from
the heightened expectations of Christmas. Here are a
few ideas:

- Meet up at a local coffee shop
- Make popcorn and watch old movies
- Put something in the slow cooker
- Organize a treasure hunt

- Fly kites on the beach
- Paint a wall with blackboard paint and ask everyone to contribute to a giant chalk mural
- Visit a museum or a beautiful garden
- Drop a coin on a local map and go where it lands
- Take blankets outside and watch the moon and stars
- Invite the neighbors round to drink the last of the mulled wine
- Reflect on Christmas together, and discuss what you might do differently next year

A MINI-BREAK

If winter is getting you down, a short break might be just the tonic you need. If this is appealing, consider departing from a small local airport and packing light to minimize stress.

If you love the idea but can't afford to go, or don't want the hassle of a long journey, try rediscovering your local area. Rent an Airbnb for a night or two and choose where to roam on a whim: pick a random place name or head for green space on the map. Take bikes, outdoor clothes and boots, and a notebook. Leave your alarm clock and to-do list at home.

How to Minimize Stress Between Christmas and New Year ❄

Where possible . . .

- Stay away from shopping malls and online sales
- Stay out of your inbox
- Avoid mindless scrolling on social media
- Keep your distance from loud, aggressive people
- Go easy on alcohol and sugar
- Avoid making too many plans: light and loose is the theme of the week
- Avoid traveling to busy places if possible; if you must, take earphones and a good book

---

MULLED APPLE AND MEMORIES

This is the perfect time to reflect on Christmas. Taking stock while the festivities are fresh in your mind—either alone or with your loved ones—will give you a clear, accurate picture of what actually took place, so you can make any changes well in advance next year.

CALM CONTEMPLATION:
REFLECTING ON CHRISTMAS

Either answer the following questions directly or use them as prompts to help your thoughts flow freely. Be specific and totally honest.

- Which single moment did you enjoy most this Christmas? Which was your least favorite?
- Which aspect of the preparations did you enjoy most? Which was your least favorite?
- What was especially stressful?
- What was especially tiring?

- What was especially fun?
- What was especially magical?
- When did you feel most calm?
- When did you experience joy?
- What surprised you?
- What felt like a waste of time, energy, or money?
- Which of your efforts were really appreciated?
- How did you show your loved ones that you love them?
- Whose presence was challenging?
- Who was a delight?
- If you made any changes to Christmas this year compared to previous years, how did they work out, for you and others?
- What are you glad you did, even if you did not enjoy it at the time, perhaps because of particular circumstances?
- What did you do for yourself over Christmas?
- Do you have more or less energy now than you did before Christmas?
- Is your mood higher or lower now than it was before Christmas?
- What would you like to do differently next year?

CHAPTER 8

Reflecting

A LITTLE PONDERING
GOES A LONG WAY

So, here we are, in the quiet moments before the turn of the year. It's a natural time for reflection. But we must proceed with care. Depending on the kind of year we have had, unstructured reflection can lead us down the road of wallowing and regret as we think about missed opportunities, disappointments, strained relationships, and all the other challenges life has thrown our way. By contrast, constructive reflection enables us to learn from those same experiences and guides us towards a more hopeful New Year.

Taking stock in a meaningful way also highlights the goodness, love, and beauty that are already present in our lives. The contentment that arises from this knowledge will be a good friend throughout the upcoming year.

For the last decade or so, my husband and I have set aside time during the Hush to review the previous year and plan for the next. We do this individually, then bring our respective thoughts to the kitchen table over a bottle of wine, or next to a roaring fire in a country pub, and talk them through. Before I met Mr. K, I did my own version of this each year, using it as an opportunity to check in with myself, recalibrate, and sometimes change course.

Our priorities have evolved over the years, but this is always when we have some of our deepest, most candid discussions about life, marriage, family, work, where and how we live, what we are building, and how we are doing. Almost every major decision we have made since we met can be traced back to the conversations we have had during the Hush.

Now it's your turn. Together we will reflect constructively on the year gone by, then use that information to visualize where you want to go in the future and how to progress in ways that will nurture your well-being, build your confidence, and carry you forward in the direction of your dreams. You can do this alone or with a partner, with an accountability buddy or with your whole family.

First, though, it's time to look briefly to the recent past. This is a three-part process:

- Mapping the year
- Reflecting
- Letting go and moving forward

Below, you will find several sets of questions that will help you squeeze all the goodness out of your experiences over the past twelve months and extract helpful information from the challenges you faced.

Visit your favorite café, order a pot of coffee, and sit by a window, or pack this book into a rucksack and take it for a long hike. Do whatever works for you. The important thing is to make a start.

A word of warning: you will probably find some of the questions quite difficult. But just take it easy, be honest, and don't give yourself a hard time. Take as long as you need. Do a little today and a little tomorrow, if you prefer. Allow your thoughts to spill onto the page uncensored, and really listen to what your inner voice has to say. You will soon learn that you are your own best guide. Don't judge yourself. Look for patterns. Keep track of how you feel as everything comes pouring out. Your emotions are a clue to what matters most to you. If you find anything too hard to handle on your own, try talking it over with a friend or reach out for professional support.

MAPPING THE YEAR

A lot can happen in a year, good and bad. We are all juggling so many commitments, obligations, and responsibilities that it can sometimes pass by in a blur. December can come around again before we know it. And when we do reflect on what has happened, we often focus exclusively on the highest highs and the lowest lows, while neglecting the subtle, nuanced ebbs and flows of everyday life that comprise the vast majority of our experiences each year.

This exercise is all about understanding what really happened last year and learning how it affected your mood and confidence, while honoring the past twelve months of life.

- First, draw out the table below in your notebook. Along the top row, write the header "Theme," followed by the months of the year. Now, in the left-hand column, write "Home," "Work," "Change," "Growth," "Ups," and "Downs" in each of the six remaining rows.

Theme	JAN	FEB	MAR	APR	MAY	JUN
Home						
Work						
Change						
Growth						
Ups						
Downs						

Theme	JUL	AUG	SEP	OCT	NOV	DEC
Home						
Work						
Change						
Growth						
Ups						
Downs						

- Fill in the Home and Work rows with any milestones and major events that fit in these two categories. Refer to your calendar if it helps, or flip through the photos on your phone, but don't spend too much time on this. Keep the notes really short, and don't feel as if you have to write something under every month. The idea is to create a snapshot of your year, not a detailed summary.

- Next, add some short notes relating to any important changes to your circumstances and any learning you experienced in the Change and Growth rows. Some of these will probably be connected to your entries in the Home and Work rows.

- Finally, try to remember any moments when you experienced positive and negative extremes of emotion and add these to the Ups and Downs rows. And how about any more subtle, lingering feelings at a particular point in the year? Add them, too.

Now take a look at the snapshot of your year and note where your eyes and heart are drawn. Make some notes in your journal in response to the following questions:

1. Are there any patterns of positives or negatives at certain times of the year?

2. How were you affected by major changes?

3. What personal growth was initiated by your own actions?

4. What growth was prompted by external influences?

5. How did you cope with any challenges that arose?

6. What blessings did the year bring, and how did you celebrate them?

7. How did the year feel? Did the days drag on or fly by? Did you feel like you were always running just to stand still? Or did the year have a good rhythm? Would you like more of the same in the year ahead, or a different pace?

8. Overall, how would you rate the year?

Now it's time to move on to more specific questions.

REFLECTING

Constructive reflection begins with looking at your year through a lens of grace. Imagine helping a cherished friend with this exercise: you would be kind, thoughtful, and gentle. Show yourself the same consideration.

This will enable you to find the answers that will nourish your spirit and open your heart. In turn, it will pave the way for authentic visioning ahead. View your answers as valuable information to help you move forward, not opportunities for judgment or evidence of failure.

RAPID-FIRE QUESTIONS

Write your immediate response to each of the following questions—literally the first thing that comes to mind. It may help to cover the list with a sheet of paper and move it down one line at a time, so your eyes aren't tempted to glance at what's coming next.

Over the previous twelve months, what did you:

1. Get curious about?
2. Get over?
3. Get good at?
4. Embrace?
5. Rediscover?
6. Surrender to?
7. Sacrifice?
8. Sideline?
9. Survive?
10. Celebrate?

QUESTIONS
FOR CONTEMPLATION

Approach the next two sets of questions in a different way. Refer back to your map of the year for guidance if necessary, and take a little more time over each one.

1. What did this year teach you about your capacity for courage? What risks did you take? How did they work out?

2. What did this year teach you about relationships, love, and your capacity for forgiveness?

3. What particular synchronicities did you notice?

4. Where did you bring light to the darkness for someone?

5. When were you generous, and how did that serve you?

6. Did you neglect yourself in any way? Was there a time when you did not allow yourself something you needed? If a similar situation arises this year, what will you tell yourself?

7. Of all the places where you spent time, which environment made you feel most calm? Where did you have your best ideas?

8. What changes did you notice in your loved ones?

9. What went on in the world that really affected you? What did that teach you about your role in wider society?

10. What did this year teach you about the preciousness of life?

THE PRACTICAL STUFF

This year:

1. What did you create or make happen?

2. What brought you the most satisfaction?

3. What was money well spent? And when did you waste money?

4. What was the best use of your time and energy? And where did you waste time and energy?

5. What was a real success for you? Why? What did you learn from that?

6. What didn't work out as you had hoped? Why? What did you learn from that?

7. What or who was a challenge? Why? What did you learn from that?

8. What was the single most important thing you did for your physical health?

9. What was the single most important thing you did for your mental health?

10. Looking back, if you could sum up the year in a single word, what would it be?

LETTING GO

Now that you have reflected on and analyzed this past year, it's time to let go of anything you don't want to carry with you into the next.

Tear a sheet of paper into several small pieces. Write one thing you wish to leave behind on each one.

Think about:

- particular grievances
- specific aspects of challenging relationships
- longings for things that are no longer available
- old stories that result in recurring self-destructive behavior
- attitudes that no longer fit your life
- judgments that stand in the way of connection
- habits you want to break

Take a moment to consider what you might be making room for when you let these things go.

Next, you can make a small altar from a candle and a circle of stones or other natural objects. Alternatively, you could build a bonfire. Then, one by one, burn the small pieces of paper. As you release each one, put your hand over your heart and feel the burden ebbing away. You may want to do this in silence, or give thanks for what each one has taught you. Or you could simply screw up the pieces of paper and throw them in the bin. It's the commitment to releasing them that matters.

MOVING FORWARD

As the year draws to a close, I encourage you to consider your own vulnerability. When have you allowed yourself to be vulnerable over the past twelve months, and what did you learn in the process?

My friend Sas Petherick, a self-doubt researcher, had a medical procedure last Christmas that changed so much for her, but not in the way you might expect.

Sas's mother and grandmother both had a congenital heart defect and died in their fifties. Sas has the same condition, so for years she assumed she would suffer the same fate. However, just before Christmas, she had emergency surgery and a groundbreaking robotic device was fitted to her heart. Now, her prognosis is excellent:

> It's as though there is now a line on the map of my life—a border crossing into this new territory I find myself in. My earliest memory is of my first heart surgery, and the expectation that I would only live until my fifties has long been a shadowy undercurrent. It's driven me to pack a lot in. After walking right up to the edge of everything, I've found that on the other side is not an early death, but a long life. I'm in uncharted territory. I am trying to be interested in who I am now.

I love this notion of "trying to be interested in who I am now." It's so refreshing when we spend so much of our time looking to the future and to who we might become.

For the final part of your reflecting and releasing process, take a few moments to tune in to your heart-wisdom and consider the following questions:

- What do you want to carry with you into the New Year?
- What truths are you ready to start believing?
- What are you ready to receive?

With the answers fresh in your mind, it's time to start making a plan.

CHAPTER 9

A Glimpse of Next Year

SOMETHING IS STIRRING

As December draws to a close, there is movement in the air. The year is hiking up her skirts and preparing to leave. Another twelve months have passed. Another chance for a fresh beginning is upon us. It's an excuse for a party, and perhaps a welcome opportunity to bid farewell to a difficult year.

There is something undeniably inviting about the imminent "first of the first." All around there are calls for "New Year, New You," yet again trying to lure us into unrealistic resolutions. While I love a fresh page in a new diary as much as the next person, I can't help wondering if we have made the turn of the year into something more imposing than it need be. After all, in the Gregorian calendar, introduced

227

by Pope Gregory XIII in 1582, the end of December is a rather arbitrary cutoff point, given that those of us in the northern hemisphere are still in the depths of midwinter, and our natural inclination is to hunker down and hibernate rather than embark on a bold new adventure. Nature is not bursting into life in our gardens, yet we have made a custom of aggressively shaking ourselves awake and issuing public proclamations of what we will quit or achieve.

Instead, perhaps we would be better off committing to languid dreaming, to ongoing nurture and care, and to acceptance of the fact that it's okay to wait a while before launching into something new. Maybe we would be better served by moving gently into January with grace and hope and a steaming cup of tea.

Animals have a number of different rhythms. Most of us are familiar with the circadian rhythm, which governs sleeping and waking in every twenty-four-hour cycle, but there are also circannual rhythms. According to Vinod Kumar of the University of Delhi, various circannual rhythms govern insect pupation, bird migration, mammal hibernation, fish reproduction, and so on throughout the animal kingdom. All of these evolved to ensure the survival of the species in question, since any timing errors in these crucial activities can have serious consequences for an animal's health and well-being.[1]

It's difficult to study the circannual rhythm in humans, but our fundamental animal nature makes it likely that our behavior and energy levels will also vary throughout the year. If that's the case, shouldn't we keep track of how we feel in the four seasons of the year—when we have the most energy, when we feel like resting, when we feel creative, and so on— and tailor our activities accordingly? Research suggests that both mood and energy levels peak in the spring and summer, whereas sleep demands are greatest in the middle of winter.[2]

I try to align my plans with my energy levels and natural flow through the seasons. These three guiding principles should help you make a calm entrance into the New Year:

1. **Don't try to reinvent yourself**. Ignore the "New Year, New You" pressure. You are perfectly imperfect just as you are. Instead, acknowledge where you are on

your personal path. Find the real truth beneath your vision for a different version of your life.

2. **Don't make false promises or random, unrealistic resolutions.** Nothing permanent is built on January 1. So avoid making overenthusiastic commitments at the very start of the year. Instead, dream, scheme, and ease yourself in. Assess the amount of energy you have for the coming year, and pledge to remain open to new ideas.

3. **Plan loosely, for the time being.** Promise to check in with yourself in a few weeks' time to decide when the real action will begin, and what it should entail. For now, though, give your ideas a chance to percolate. Explore. Make notes. Once you are ready to sketch out the whole year, align your proposed activities with the seasons, or the moon, or your own natural rhythm.

NEW YEAR'S REVOLUTION

During the course of your life, you can reinvent yourself as many times as you like. You can keep adding whole chapters to your story, or a paragraph here and a sentence there. It's up to you. There are no rules, and certainly not one that says you must tear up the whole manuscript and start again every time the New Year bells toll. The process of creating meaningful change is far more nuanced than that.

All too often, goal setting on January 1 involves plucking ambitious targets out of thin air in the hope that they will motivate us off the sofa. By its nature, a New Year's resolution is a recipe for either success or failure, and that's a lot of pressure when you're just emerging from the sugar-and-alcohol-induced coma of Christmas. So, it's hardly surprising that they rarely work.

The word "resolution" and its sister verb "resolve" provide a clue to what's wrong with the whole concept. We attempt to "re-solve" the same old problems in a short burst of activity each and every January, which results in a perennial cycle of beating ourselves up.

Any commitment to change that is not connected to a soul-deep, genuine need or—crucially—based in hope is unlikely to stick. Yet, every time we abandon one of our resolutions, we fail a little in our own eyes.

So, rather than focusing exclusively on the New Year, why not make a change simply because it's a new day? Do it because you are fed up with living how others tell you to live. Do it because you know what you really need, and because you know you need to begin. You can start any time, and restart any time.

This year, I am proposing a New Year's *revolution*. Besides being a dynamic and powerful call to arms, the word "revolution"—from the Latin *revolvere* ("roll back")—invites us to sweep away the layers of expectation, worry, conformity, convention, even comfort and see what is waiting to be born this year. Instead of making random resolutions, we will practice nourishing rituals. Instead of setting ourselves unrealistic goals, we will articulate beautiful dreams, then work out how to bring them to life.

VISIONING

What are you being called to journey towards? It's important to have some sense of that before deciding what to commit to this year, so you can use your resources to bring your dreams to life. I am not asking you to decide on one particular thing you want to achieve, but rather to imagine a particular version of your life—which could be slightly, or radically, different from your life today—and imagine what that might feel like. This is the essence of your dream.

For example, you might feel called towards writing for a living. That doesn't just mean getting a book published (which would be the kind of single achievement we tend to focus on) but all that goes with that kind of life—respecting your own talent, spending your days pondering big questions, playing with language, inspiring others, enjoying quiet time and deep thought, and feeling connected to a treasured community of creative people.

At any point in time, a dreamer like you or me could be at one of eight possible positions in the Dream Development Process.

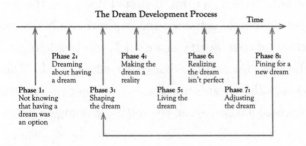

The Dream Development Process

Time

Phase 1: Not knowing that having a dream was an option

Phase 2: Dreaming about having a dream

Phase 3: Shaping the dream

Phase 4: Making the dream a reality

Phase 5: Living the dream

Phase 6: Realizing the dream isn't perfect

Phase 7: Adjusting the dream

Phase 8: Pining for a new dream

Not only are we all at different stages of this process at any given moment, but it takes each of us different amounts of time, effort, and confidence to move through the phases. Some of us may blast through one, then linger in the next. Others may dither at the border of two phases, unsure whether to move forward.

New Year visioning is all about working out your current position in the Dream Development Process, and deciding the action you need to take to move forward. This is a six-step procedure.

STEP 1:
ACKNOWLEDGE YOUR DREAM

First, you must acknowledge the dream you are working towards. Remember, by "dream" I don't mean a particular tangible achievement, but rather a particular version of your life. If you are stuck, try completing the sentence, "I want to be living a life where . . ." or "I am being called towards life as a . . ." As you complete the sentence, imagine what you might be doing on a day-to-day basis, how you spend your time and energy, how you earn money, how you feel, how you connect with others, and so on. Paint a picture in your mind, or on paper if it helps.

Your dream might be life as a digital nomad with your partner, working freelance as you move from one tropical island to another on a whim, having left the rat race far behind. Or it might be living a slower life with your family on a small farm, miles away from shopping malls and traffic, selling your wares at a friendly local farmers' market each Saturday and spending Sunday afternoons cooking up feasts for your friends. Or it might simply be living a life where you aren't running on empty from morning until night.

Whatever it is, this process will help you realize your dream.

STEP 2:
FIGURE OUT WHERE YOU ARE
IN TERMS OF REALIZING THAT DREAM

Take another look at the Dream Development Process diagram and identify the phase that best correlates with your current situation.

Most visioning exercises presume you are conjuring an idea from scratch, but in reality the outline of your dream probably started to form some time ago. Indeed, it might have entered your consciousness during childhood or your earlier adult years, and you might have cultivated the idea for a while before suppressing it later in life.

Perhaps you recognized your dream at some point in the past and then tried to bring it to fruition. If so, you might now be in a consolidation phase, taking a break before pressing on, or possibly adjusting your vision to suit new circumstances or different priorities.

Or you may have spent many years building something that no longer seems as appealing as it once did, and you are ready to try something else.

236

Dream development can be intimidating if you think your dream is out of reach. So, remind yourself that it's a long-term process. Rather than asking, "How can I make my dream come true?" it might be more helpful to ask: "What will be this year's contribution to my Dream Development?" Spend some time figuring out practical actions you can take in the coming months.

Of course, you might conclude that major work is needed this year. On the other hand, a little extra consistency might enable you to progress to the next phase. Or a few small tweaks here and there. Some research. More interactions with like-minded people. More confidence in your own ability.

Sometimes a few small changes are enough to initiate the shift towards your dream.

The quality and authenticity of your dream are paramount. Are you picturing what you think you *should* want, or what you truly want? Are you listening to what others urge you to do or following your own heart?

CLARITY IS OVERRATED

Trying to construct your vision too rigidly can be limiting. Rather than painting a still life, look for shapes in the moving clouds of your mind. We have to nurture our dreams tenderly, and allow them the time and space to reveal themselves. That's what January is for.

Imagine you have already decided to take a leap. How does it feel? Tell a few trusted friends (not too many). Do some research. Explore ways to make it happen. Meditate on it. Write about it. Swirl it around in your mind. Take your time. Sketch it out loosely. Let it evolve.

Traditional goal setting requires absolute clarity and measurable targets. But life is fluid and floaty, so you really need courage and commitment, along with some broad themes and dreams, rather than every last detail. If you can embrace not knowing, and are flexible enough to shape and adapt as you go, you'll uncover more wonder than you could possibly imagine.

I am not advocating the complete abandonment of goal setting. Goals can be useful guideposts to help you move along the phases in the Dream Development Process. But ultimately what matters is the kind of life you want to live, because that will determine the quality and richness of your day-to-day experience.

Sometimes the path you choose will render a particular (minor) goal obsolete. If you are obsessed with that goal, you might waste time and energy pursuing it beyond its usefulness, or consider yourself a failure for not achieving it. By contrast, you'll have no trouble letting it go along the way if your focus is on advancing towards the bigger picture of your dream.

STEP 3:
LOOK FOR A QUICKER WAY

Dutch philosopher and psychologist Gijs Deckers once said, "The sense of satisfaction lies not in having a beautiful farmhouse but in the things you do there: enjoy a cup of coffee or read a book in the garden."[3]

This highlights a crucial point: we often think we want something specific, but it's actually what the thing *represents* that we yearn for. If you can figure out what your "dream" really represents, you will likely uncover many different paths towards it, and ways to bring it to life sooner than you thought.

For instance, let's stick with the example of the beautiful farmhouse. What is it about that house that is so appealing? If you want it because you love the idea of growing your own organic vegetables, you could join a community garden. If it's the environment that is appealing, try renting a cozy cottage for a week for your own private retreat. If it actually represents freedom of time, you could try negotiating a four-day workweek to have Fridays to yourself. Maybe you will eventually end up living in a beautiful farmhouse, or maybe instead you will bring to life what it represents in another way.

Growth is rarely linear. Sometimes you'll feel energized and inspired, or motivated by desperation. At other times you'll feel so burnt out that you can barely get through the day, never mind commit to a major change.

STEP 4:
TAKE RADICAL ACTION

That said, it can be empowering to take radical action to help you realize your dream. This is not about scale, but boldness. It's about doing something outside of your comfort zone—something that feels scary but exciting.

STEP 5:
ALIGN WITH THE SEASONS

Look at the year ahead and make a plan based on the seasons. Consider the energy you have at different times of the year as well as the amount of light and the weather, if these will restrict your actions. Think about your mood and your natural tendencies from one season to the next. Ideally, choose one goal for each season to serve as a guidepost on the path to your dream.

STEP 6:
LET IT GO

Now, after all that thinking about your dream, it's time to let it go. *Really!* It can be powerful to think about your intention carefully, then just let it go. This allows the magic to happen. Note that "letting go" is not synonymous with "giving up." Rather, it means loosening your grip so your dream is free to take its own shape.

CALM CONTEMPLATION:
ARE YOU READY?

Now is a good time to assess your readiness for the year ahead and consider ways to prepare yourself:

- What if this will end up being the most transformational year you have ever experienced? Are you ready?
- What if this is going to be a really hard year? Are you ready?

242

- What if your health will be challenged this year? Are you ready?
- What if you are going to meet a wonderful new friend this year? Are you ready?
- What if everything is going to change due to a major shift in the world? Are you ready?

CLEARING A PATH

I used to plan carefully, scheduling my life to maximize every minute in my week. But these days I do the opposite, first planning in space for who-knows-what (because we never know what opportunities are around the corner). It may sound counterintuitive, but the busier I am, the more important this becomes.

If you fancy giving it a try, be warned—it can be very uncomfortable, because the pages of a diary almost beg to be filled up. First, in go all the family commitments, then the working hours, then the social events, then the exercise routine. Finally, if we're lucky, there may be a bit of space around the edges to pencil in a few minutes to work on our dreams. Week in, week out, it's always the same. So, if any exciting, unexpected opportunities come along, they have to be squeezed into an already packed schedule, which is sure to limit the quality of our work or have a detrimental impact on our well-being.

I dare you to flip all of that on its head and begin with the spaces instead. It is a straightforward two-step process:

1. Take an annual calendar, block out some large chunks of time, and label them "Unknown Goodness Coming My Way." It may be that you can block out a whole month over the summer, or perhaps you can only manage a week at this point. Perhaps it is easier for you to block out a few days each quarter, or a day a month. Depending on whether you have your own business, work for someone else, are a stay-at-home parent, etc., the extent to which you can do this will vary, but the more time you can block out, the better.

2. Trust.

That's it.

It's uncanny how often something wonderful turns up to fill the space you've reserved. Indeed, it seems to happen every single time I do it. Even if nothing particular comes along, you win anyway because you've blocked out some precious time to work towards your dream, exercise your creativity, focus on something new, or even just take a break from your usual routine.

Another version of this exercise involves reserving smaller chunks of time for dream work on a more regular basis, such as weekly. This should be scheduled in before everything else, and you must protect it fiercely. The bigger the chunks of time, the better. A whole day is a treasure, and a single block of two hours is more conducive to productive work than four half-hours scattered throughout the week, although if that's all you can spare, it's a good place to start.

Remember, lack of time is rarely the real problem. Rather, instead of focusing on what really matters, we waste time procrastinating and attending to insignificant details. When we schedule time to open up space for new possibilities and to work on our dreams, things begin to take shape.

If you have a partner, encourage them to go through

the process with you, so you can support each other's dreams. Try to find a way to honor them together, and build the shared life you both crave.

If you follow these simple steps, you can look ahead with enthusiasm, without pushing yourself too hard. They will enable you to work towards your dreams without sacrificing your well-being or allowing self-doubt to sabotage your plans. Be sure to allocate some recovery time after any major change or effort. This will enable you to recharge your batteries and keep the momentum. Finally, reflect often and amend your dreams as you go.

Hopefully this will help you enjoy an even more joyful Christmas next year, as you celebrate all that has gone before.

This leads us to our final journaling exercise.

CALM CONTEMPLATION:
YOUR INTENTIONS FOR THE YEAR AHEAD

Based on everything you have written in your journal and swirled around in your mind, answer the following questions about the year ahead:

- What do you want more of this coming year? What are you willing to trade, forgo, or sacrifice to get it?
- What do you want less of? How will you ensure that happens?
- What specific project or idea is demanding your attention right now? How will you make time for it?
- What do you need to learn, or work on, this year?
- How will you steady yourself in times of inevitable uncertainty?
- Who do you want to spend more time with? And who do you want to spend less time with?
- What is your definition of living well? Which

247

attitudes, habits, rituals, and rhythms will help you live that way?

- What are you hopeful about?
- What is your overall intention for the coming year?

LUCKY NOODLES
AND CHAMPAGNE TOASTS

It's Millennium Eve in Tokyo. I'm hopping from bar to bar with a bunch of friends. We eat toshikoshi soba *("over-the-year noodles") to mark the transition from one year to the next, and express our gratitude for various good things in a series of toasts. We start off small, but by midnight we are toasting life, the universe, and everything.*

We make our way to the beach at Enoshima and watch the year 2000 dawn in the Land of the Rising Sun. The locals have built bonfires on the sand, and some are dancing or swimming. There is a joyful relief in the air—that we have made it into a new millennium and that we are here in this glorious place, looking out to sea, celebrating at the edge of everything.

The beach begins to empty as the flames die down, and we follow the crowd for hatsumōde—*the first shrine visit of the year. The queue spirals around the hillside, and people are dozing where they stand. We drink warm, milky sake and phone home to wish happy New Year to our families many time zones away. Then we catch the slow train home, to sleep.*

For some, New Year's Eve is the highlight of the year. I have dressed up and gotten drunk and kissed strangers at midnight just like anyone else. And I'll never forget the year an old friend got married on a beach in Thailand, his bride arriving on an elephant. We sent Chinese lanterns into the sky and feasted until morning.

These days, though, I have a different approach to the New Year gateway. I prefer to bid farewell to the old year with a simple ritual of candles and a few words. Then I rise early on January 1, stretch, and offer a quiet blessing with a sense of gratitude and a word of hope.

> *Good morning, world.*
> *Happy New Year.*

I prefer to step into the new day with a clear head and a good breakfast. Then I like to walk the land, to feel it under my feet and reconnect with the miracle of another year on this spinning planet.

This year, I squelched through mud, my old leather boots squeaking with each step. There is no sunshine to rival that which beats down from a crisp blue sky on a cold winter's day. I listened for the sounds of January: water dripping into the gutter; birds singing near the disused railway; streams bubbling; wind in the trees. I passed one village after another at a steady pace, the white signposts like markers in time and place and possibility. A few fields over, an engine rumbled as someone blew away the cobwebs in their vintage sports car.

Gift yourself a gentle January this year. There are many ways to ease yourself into the month. You could practice twelve days of gratitude, take long walks, catch up with friends, dream and plan. Linger on the things you love, and seek joy outdoors. If the darkness weighs heavy, go back to Chapter 3 and nourish yourself through it. Perhaps you might close out the festive season with a Twelfth Night feast.

MOVING FORWARD WITH HOPE

As you move into January, carry the themes of the Five Stories of Christmas with you, but now apply them to daily life. If you like, redraw your Christmas Constellation as a Life Constellation, mapping out how much you value Faith, Magic, Connection, Abundance, and Heritage not just at Christmas but every day. Then, as you move through each day, and through the year, make sure you honor them with your decisions, heart, and attention.

All of life is a story. Myths and legends. Folklore and fairy tales. Imagination and memory. Diaries and dinner dates. Catch-ups over a pint and family chats around the kitchen table. Fact and fiction. Hope and expectation. Truth and dream. Each detail a sentence, each conversation a page.

This is the story of *your* life, my friend. Live it fully. Write it well.

Believe in Magic

It's February, and I am lying in the dark while the rest of my family sleeps. For some reason, I'm thinking about my younger daughter Maia's quirky Christmas list, which read like this:

1. *A teddy*
2. *A real pig*
3. *Diamonds*
4. *Batman socks for Daddy*
5. *Snow*

I am just thinking how it was so like her to include a present for someone else, when I hear a tumble of footsteps. Maia comes running into our room, curly hair wild, eyes full of the dream she has just had.

"Mummy, there was a noise on the roof and I go up to

see and it was Santa and Elfie and it was cold. I not have my slippers."

"Really? Did they see you?"

"Yes! They ask me to help them. The sleigh big and green and full of . . ."

"Presents?"

"Snow! We throw it off the roof and it make the garden white!"

"What a wonderful dream," I say, kissing her on the forehead as I get out of bed and wander over to the window.

"Elfie come back in the midnight!" she insists, pulling at my pajamas in her eagerness to convince me that Santa's favorite elf returned to our home last night. "I see him, Mummy."

Smiling, I open the curtains to welcome the morning, turn to the window . . . and gasp. We have had the first snowfall of the year.

Perhaps there is such a thing as Christmas magic, after all . . .

Acknowledgments

Writing about Christmas feels like a tremendous responsibility. I am immensely grateful to the many people who have helped me bring this book to life. Hundreds of people shared their Christmas memories with me, and I am particularly indebted to those who allowed me to share their stories.

Christmas is complicated, so I am grateful to the scholarly work of many, as listed in the bibliography at dowhatyouloveforlife.com/course/cc, and in particular Daniel Miller's *Unwrapping Christmas*, an excellent collection of anthropological essays that pointed me in the direction of many further sources of historical information. Judith Flanders's *Christmas: A Biography* also offered a fresh perspective that made me question many of my own assumptions about Christmas.

I also want to offer particular thanks to Michael

Danks of the Forestry Commission in the New Forest, Hampshire, for his advice, and to Alan Buckingham and his book *Allotment Month By Month*, for the seasonal growing facts.

Further thanks go to Horatio Clare, for showing me how to write about winter and reminding me to sometimes think like a nine-year-old, to Bella Bathurst for her laser insight, and to Rebecca Campbell and Will Storr for unknowingly blowing it all apart and bringing it back together. I am grateful to Pico Iyer for the kind words, to Arthur Golden for returning my call, and to Lucy Brazier for the chats and the Bramley apple-lemon curd recipe. Lastly, I must thank Sarah McLachlan for her beautiful album *Wintersong*, which I listened to on repeat while writing.

I raise a glass of Christmas cheer to my wonderful agent Caroline Hardman, to the brilliant Thérèse Coen for getting my words out in the world in many languages, and to the whole team at Hardman & Swainson.

I am hugely grateful to the whole team at Piatkus, and in particular to Jillian Young, Jillian Stewart, Phillip Parr, Emily Courdelle, Beth Wright, and Aimee Kitson. In the US, my deepest gratitude lies with Kara Watson of Scribner, who sprinkled magic over these pages from her desk at Rockefeller Center in New York City, home of that iconic skating rink and giant Christmas tree.

This book was mostly written at my kitchen table, but would never have been finished without time and space, and good coffee, for which I am indebted to Karl and the team at The Lyme Bay (Lyme Regis), Steve and Elaine at Amid Giants & Idols (Lyme Regis), Jerry & Wendy's place, the hideaway on Rousdon Estate, Arvon at Totleigh Barton, and Gemma for her sweet place in Frome. I owe a stockingful of thanks to my in-laws, Joan and Bob Kempton, and to all the lovely friends who invited my family to tea while I was busy writing.

My own Christmas memories would not be what they are without the magical experiences my parents created for my brothers and me when we were young, and for that I will be forever grateful. These days, I am happy that the Christmas celebrations have grown to include the joy of our nieces and nephews—Will, Holly, Freya, Finley, Zack, Grace, Cody, and Kinsley.

ACKNOWLEDGMENTS

Most of all, my heart lies with my husband, Mr. K, who makes it all possible and special, and my daughters, Sienna and Maia, who light up our daily lives with their magic. You are my greatest gift, at Christmas and all year round.

Endnotes, Bibliography, and Bonus Content

To save paper, the endnotes, bibliography, and all bonus content have been made available online as follows:

Endnotes: bethkempton.com/calmchristmas/
   endnotesusa/
Bibliography: bethkempton.com/calmchristmas/
   bibliography
Templates: bethkempton.com/calmchristmas/
   templates

About the Author

Beth Kempton is an award-winning entrepreneur and author, whose books have been translated into twenty-four languages. She teaches and writes about doing what you love and living well. Her first book, *Freedom Seeker: Live More. Worry Less. Do What You Love.*, is an uplifting manual for feeling free. Beth's second book, *Wabi Sabi: Japanese Wisdom for a Perfectly Imperfect Life*, holds a wealth of valuable life lessons extracted from centuries-old Japanese culture and aesthetics. Beth has a master's degree in Japanese and is a dedicated student of Japanese life.

Her third book, *We Are in This Together: Finding Hope and Opportunity in the Depths of Adversity*, is a guide for coping with Covid-19. Together with her husband, Beth runs three different businesses—dowhatyouloveforlife.com, makeartthatsells.com, and makeitindesign.com—all of which offer tools, resources, and online courses for living an inspired life.

The mother of two adorable daughters, Beth lives a slowish life in Devon, England, and has been obsessed with Christmas since she was a little girl. You can take a peek at her perfectly imperfect life on Instagram @bethkempton.

FIND BETH HERE:

www.bethkempton.com / www.dowhatyouloveforlife
.com
Instagram: @bethkempton
Facebook: www.facebook.com/dowhatyoulovexx
Twitter: @dowhatyoulovexx
Podcast: bethkempton.com/podcast

ONLINE COURSES:

Do What You Love
How to be Happy (and Calm, Organised + Focused)
Reach Teach Profit: The E-course Creation Masterclass
The Book Proposal Masterclass

For more information about courses, please visit dowhatyouloveforlife.com.